THE GOSPELS TODAY

THE GOSPELS TODAY

CHALLENGING READINGS OF JOHN, MARK, LUKE & MATTHEW

ESSENTIAL INQUIRIES, VOLUME 2

STEPHEN W. NEED

COWLEY PUBLICATIONS
Lanham, Chicago, New York, Toronto, and Plymouth, UK

Published by Cowley Publications
An imprint of Rowman & Littlefield Publishers, Inc.
A wholly owned subsidiary of
The Rowman & Littlefield Publishing Group, Inc.
4501 Forbes Boulevard, Suite 200
Lanham, MD 20706

Estover Road
Plymouth PL6 7PY
United Kingdom

Distributed by National Book Network

Library of Congress Cataloging-in-Publication Data

Need, Stephen W. (Stephen William), 1957–
The Gospels today : challenging readings of John, Mark, Luke, and Matthew / Stephen W. Need.
p. cm. — (Essential inquiries ; v. 2)
Includes bibliographical references and index.
ISBN-13: 978-1-56101-297-8 (pbk. : alk. paper)
ISBN-10: 1-56101-297-1 (pbk. : alk. paper)
1. Bible. N.T. Gospels—Criticism, interpretation, etc. I. Title. II. Series.
BS2555.52.N44 2007
226'.06—dc22 2007013756

Printed in the United States of America.

∞™ The paper used in this publication meets the minimum requirements of American National Standard for Information Sciences—Permanence of Paper for Printed Library Materials, ANSI/NISO Z39.48-1992.

For Leslie Houlden
In gratitude

CONTENTS

INTRODUCTION

The Gospels Today: Challenging Readings of John, Mark, Luke & Matthew and its companion volume, *Paul Today: Challenging Readings of Acts and the Epistles*, have arisen out of my teaching New Testament Studies in various institutions in England and to groups in the Holy Land, Greece, and Turkey over a period of more than twenty-five years. Both volumes are designed to enable students and other interested readers to get a quick overview of a number of issues or problems in the areas concerned. Together, the chapters present a profile or silhouette of issues that arise in studying a text or theme from Paul or the Gospels. They show the range of concerns that arise from a particular New Testament text or theme to give you, the reader, a working knowledge of what's at stake in trying to understand and interpret a particular text or problem, and, I hope, to stimulate you to do further reading on topics and texts that interest you particularly. But there is more than this. Taken together, the chapters demonstrate different ways of approaching New Testament texts and issues. For example, they show how historical and theological questions play a part in understanding a text; how exegetical issues can make serious differences; how matters relating to ancient Judaism and the Greco-Roman world have a place in interpreting these texts for us today; how questions of language are crucial; how archaeology can illumine a text; and how patristic and other interpretations of texts might have obscured an author's intentions. So together the chapters show how a number of academic disciplines and concerns are

Each chapter is complete in itself and can be read independently of the others, and the individual chapters can be read in any order. The views expressed here are my own and do not represent any institution or organization.

I would like to thank Professor Leslie Houlden for reading an early draft of this book and my wife Jill Dampier for checking the final manuscript. Any remaining errors are my own responsibility.

Stephen W. Need
Jerusalem
June 2006

ONE

REREADING THE PROLOGUE
INCARNATION AND CREATION IN JOHN 1:1–18

The Prologue to St. John's Gospel is one of the most widely known and frequently read texts of the New Testament. Its famous claim that "the Word became flesh and dwelt among us" (1:14) is familiar to Christians the world over. For centuries, the Roman Mass ended with the so-called "last Gospel," which was usually a reading (whether privately or aloud) of John 1:1–14. In most churches today, as in the past, the main Gospel reading at Christmas is John 1:1–14. And as elsewhere, the annual Christmas carol service at King's College Cambridge—broadcast around the world—comes to a dramatic climax with the reading of this text.

For most Christians, of course, the belief that the eternal Word of God was made flesh in Jesus of Nazareth comprises the very essence of Christian faith itself. However, in spite of its popularity, a full appreciation of the theology of John's Prologue is rare. A number of factors have contributed to this state of affairs: a general lack of awareness of the background and meaning of the word *logos*; interpreting the words "He was in the world" and "He came to his own home" (vv. 10–11) as if they referred to the

Logos incarnate in Jesus, rather than to the Logos in creation; and the common liturgical practice of reading only to verse 14 instead of to verse 18 of John 1.

In this chapter, I first discuss the background and meaning of the word *logos* in Jewish and Greek thought; second, I show how the theological and literary structure of the Prologue emphasizes the activity of the Logos in creation more than is usually admitted; and finally, I make some brief concluding comments underlining the fundamental theological connection between the incarnation and creation. My overall aim is to show that the Logos is by definition active in creation and that this is an important part of the theology of the incarnation in John's Prologue. Too much emphasis on the incarnation of the Logos in Jesus in John 1:14 has sometimes obscured the equally important emphasis on the prior activity of the Logos in creation in the preceding verses.

The Meaning of Logos in Jewish and Greek Thought

The fundamental connection in John 1:1–18 between God's activity in his incarnation in Jesus and his prior activity in creation can be seen most clearly through an understanding of the notion of the Logos. The word *logos* and the concepts associated with it were subsequently to become crucial to the christological formulations of the great councils of the church. But what would this word have meant to the original readers of John's Prologue? By far the most common translation of *logos* in John 1 is "word," although this has its limitations if it is thought of only as speech. The background of the word *logos* is broad and complex, but important connotations and associations from Jewish and Greek use (often lost in subsequent Christian use) bear substantially upon its meaning here in John's Prologue. As we shall see, in ancient Jewish thought *logos* did have to do with the active "speech" of God, whereas in Greek thought it was used much more broadly of the rational element that ordered the universe. In later Christian thought, for example in the theology of Athanasius in the fourth century, Logos came more clearly to mean a personal rational element, a part of the triune God, which ordered and governed the universe and which became incarnated in Jesus. In earlier Greek philosophy it was already thought of more as "rationality" than as "speech," although "discourse" was also part of the meaning.

Of course, the idea that a god was present and active in his word in creation and in history can already be found in many of the religious traditions of the ancient Near East, and there is nothing unique about its appearance in the Israelite, Greek, and Christian traditions. However, I limit the discussion here to the cultures that bore specifically upon the usage in John's Prologue, namely, those of Israel and Greece. A glance at the Hebrew Bible and at the Greek philosophy of the Stoics will reveal the roots of the essential connection between incarnation and creation in John's Prologue.

In ancient Israel, the expression "the word of God" was essentially a metaphor for God's activity in creation and history. The Hebrew equivalent to *logos* is *dabar* and, as in the Greek, the associated Hebrew verbs do mean "speaking" or "saying." But the metaphor of the "word of God" already signified something more than simply words. It signified the dynamic activity by which God communicated to his people and revealed his nature and will to them.

Among the best examples of the basic idea here are the communications of God to the prophets of Israel who frequently use the expression "the word of the Lord." Jeremiah, for example, writes, "Now the word of the Lord came to me saying, 'Before I formed you in the womb I knew you'" (Jer. 1:4f.; cf. Is. 9:8; Ezek. 1:3; Hos. 1:1; Amos 3.1). The notion of "God speaking" in creation was already present in the Genesis narrative: "And God said" (e.g., 1:3, 6, 9). For the Psalmist, the "word" was the instrument of creation itself: "By the word of the Lord the heavens were made, and all their host by the breath of his mouth" (Ps. 33:6). The "word" was also sometimes thought of as having its own independent existence in the purposes of God (Is. 55:10–11).

The "word of the Lord" in ancient Israelite thinking, therefore, was not only a matter of speech. It was a metaphor for God's dynamic, active communication of his nature and will to his people and was specifically associated with his act of creation. In the Septuagint or LXX, the Greek translation of the Hebrew Bible, the Hebrew word *dabar* is almost always translated as *logos*.

It is also clear that another tradition in the theology of ancient Israel bore upon John's use of the word *logos* in his Prologue, and was also to become central to early Christian theology. That other tradition is "wisdom" or in Hebrew *hokmah*, usually associated with such literature as the books of Proverbs, Job, Ecclesiastes, Ecclesiasticus, and the Wisdom of Solomon. Wisdom or *hokma* was closely related conceptually to *dabar* (e.g., Wisd. of Sol. 9:1). The wisdom tradition in ancient Israel is long and complex. Arising out of practical everyday human experience, *hokmah* had to do first of all with sayings that summed up general aspects of life, e.g., "A wise son makes a glad father, but a foolish son is a sorrow to his mother" (Prov. 10:1). In this sense wisdom had to do with morality and right living. But it also came to be personified as a beautiful woman with her own specific role in God's purposes. Some commentators have even claimed that wisdom gradually came to be thought of as a separate and distinct part of God's being. In any case, the "lady wisdom" is God's own wisdom and as such has a special role in God's relation to creation. In Proverbs 8, she is pre-existent, the first of God's acts of creation, and is also associated with God's creative power: "The Lord by wisdom founded the earth" (Prov. 3:19; cf. 8:22–31). Like the Logos of John's Prologue, wisdom permeates and orders creation (Wisd. 1:7; 8:1); is associated with life and light (Prov. 8:35; Wisd. 7:26); is spoken of as an only son (Prov. 4:3); and is rejected by humankind (Prov. 1:24–25; cf. 1 Enoch 42). In the Septuagint, or LXX, the Greek word for the lady wisdom is *sophia*, a word often thought of as the feminine equivalent of the masculine *logos*.

In the Greek tradition, the notion of *logos* was extremely powerful and pervasive. Although there were different notions and emphases, the main thrust of meaning was rather different from that in ancient Israel. In Greek thought, *logos* had to do with rationality and discourse, and this certainly included speech. The focus, however, was much broader and extended to the whole business of orderliness in the universe. In the deterministic philosophy of the Stoics, for example, *logos* was essentially the rationality or order that held the universe together. Insofar as human beings were concerned, there were two elements to *logos*: on the one hand there was "inward thought" (*logos endiathetos*); on the other hand there was "outward expression" or speech (*logos prophorikos*). Overall, *logos* was essentially a rational dimension that directed and governed the universe, including the lives of human beings. It was far more than simply a dynamic word; it had to do with the very nature and structure of creation.

By the time of the writing of John's Prologue in the first century CE, the Hebrew and Greek meanings of *dabar* and *logos* had all come together. More specifically, Judaism itself had been thoroughly Hellenized, and Hebrew words had gathered Greek meanings. In the first century CE, the marriage of Jewish and Greek thought can be seen most clearly in the thought of Philo of Alexandria. Although it is unclear whether his thinking specifically influenced the Fourth Gospel, he epitomizes the Hellenistic Jewish philosophical theology of the period. Operating in Alexandria, the great center of Hellenistic learning, Philo produced a fine synthesis of Plato's philosophy and Jewish theology. He combined all the meanings of *logos* with all the meanings of *dabar*. There is no systematic doctrine of the Logos in Philo's writings, but it is clear that he saw the Logos as fundamental to the structure of the universe and God's relation to it. For Philo, the Logos was essentially a cosmological phenomenon connected with wisdom. It was fundamentally associated with God's activity in creation, and with God's image in human beings. He also associated the Logos with the pre-existent Torah.

It was in a climate such as this that the writer of the Fourth Gospel penned his Prologue. By then, Logos was a pre-existent aspect of God's being, eternal wisdom, God's instrument of creation and vehicle of revelation, and a rational element permeating and upholding the universe. It was God's dynamic way of communicating his nature and will to his people and was by definition active in creation. The writer of the Prologue drew upon all of these meanings and claimed in addition that this Logos had been made flesh in Jesus of Nazareth.

Theological and Literary Issues in John 1:1–18

What then does the Prologue to John's Gospel actually say about the Logos? A popular understanding of the incarnation which is often read into the Prologue is that an otherwise largely absent God came to earth and was incarnated in Jesus of Nazareth. True, such a view usually acknowledges that the Logos was pre-existent, but the sole focus of this view is the incarnation of the Logos in John 1:14. The previous verses which speak of the activity of the Logos in creation are frequently overlooked. Such a view is encouraged, as I have already hinted, by liturgical readings that stop at verse 14, and also by reading verses 10–11 ("He was in the world, and the world was made through him, yet the world knew him not," and "He came to his own home, and his own people received him not") as if they refer to the Logos incarnate in Jesus coming to Israel and being rejected by the Jews. Of course, this popular view of the theology of the Prologue has been influenced by later notions of the incarnation and trinity, and also by subsequent relations between Christians and Jews. But in any case, there is much more in the Prologue about the role of the Logos in creation before its incarnation in Jesus than is usually appreciated, and as we shall see, verses 10–11 can be seen as referring much more broadly to creation and the human race, rather than simply to Israel and the Jews. A glance at the literary structure and probable history of the Prologue will help to bring this wider perspective into view.

Where does the Prologue to John's Gospel actually begin and end, and what are its key subsections? Even though some commentators have argued that John 1:1–18 is a seamless poetic narrative written at one sitting, it basically consists of two types of material: (a) verses 1–5, 9–14, and 16–18 on the Logos; and (b) verses 6–8 and 15 on John the Baptist. If these two are separated, they both make perfect sense on their own. This raises the question of whether they ever existed separately and which came first. Obviously the Prologue now begins at verse 1 and finishes either at verse 14 or at verse 18. Yet over time there has been a great deal of debate about the original ending of the Prologue. Some commentators have thought that verse 14 is the climactic ending and have also tended to overemphasize the role of the Logos in the incarnation at the expense of that in creation. Others have maintained that the Prologue continues until verse 18, returning to John the Baptist (v. 15) and to the effects of the Word made flesh upon believers after the central climax (vv. 16–18). This hasn't necessarily taken the emphasis off the incarnation in verse 14 but it has adjusted the perspective a little, enabling the overall sweep of the passage to appear more clearly with verse 14 in its proper relation to the surrounding verses.

More problematic than where the Prologue ends is the question of where the Fourth Gospel originally began and of which material originally made up the Prologue. Some commentators have claimed that the Gospel originally began, not with the Logos material as we now have it, but with verses 6–8 and 15, on John the Baptist: "There was a man sent from God whose name was John." This is certainly possible, and it is interesting to compare this with the opening of the Gospel of Mark (1:4). Such a beginning of the Fourth Gospel would then have been followed quite naturally by the later verses 19–28, the so-called "Record of John." If this is correct, it suggests that an original John the Baptist opening has later been intertwined with a "Logos hymn." Whatever the truth about the history of John 1:1–18, looking at the material separately in this way certainly helps to bring out the various emphases and especially makes verses 10–11 look rather different.

It is clear that the first readers of John's Gospel would have understood the word *logos* to mean the dynamic communicative speech of God on the one hand and the rational ordering of the universe on the other. In the minds of Johannine Christians, it would quickly evoke the pre-existent, dynamic and active, but also rational and ordering element so closely associated with God's creative activity. Recalling the opening of the book of Genesis, John 1:1 immediately underlines this connection. The relation between God and the Logos is then quickly established: in the beginning of things the Logos was with God and was God. The verse draws attention both to a unity and to a clear distinction between the two. Next, we learn that the Logos is essentially God's instrument of creation: "all things were made through him, and without him was not anything made that was made" (v. 3). The focus here is the presence and activity of the Logos in creation well before its coming in Jesus of Nazareth. The Logos, God's active Word of communication and revelation in creation and history as spoken through Israel's prophets, is next referred to as light and life (v. 5), again recalling the Genesis narrative (1:3, 24).

If we now follow the Logos material from verse 5 through to verses 9–14, an important picture emerges. The light which is the life of the Logos (vv. 4–5) and which is shining in the darkness was in the world that was made through the Logos (v. 10), as we have already been told (v. 3). "He was in the world" (v. 10), therefore, refers to the light of the Logos. The Logos is present in creation, but "the world knew him not" (v. 11). It is usually assumed that verses 10–11 refer to the coming of Jesus of Nazareth to Israel and his rejection by the Jews. In fact, on closer examination we can see that the incarnation of the Logos in Jesus has not yet occurred. We are yet to hear in verse 14 that "the Word was made flesh and dwelt among us." Although there may be an element of ambiguity here, it seems that verses 10 and 11 cannot yet refer to Jesus himself coming to Israel. Rather, the words "he was in the world" (*en to kosmo en*) and "his own home" (*ta idia*) make more sense if they are taken to refer to the Logos coming to his home in the creation which he has been so instrumental in making. The words "his own people" (*hoi idioi*) would then refer to the human race (including the Jews) which has rejected him. Only in verse 14 are we finally told that the Logos was made flesh. Verse 15 is John the Baptist material once again, while verses 16–18, the next part of the Logos hymn, tell us of the relation of Jesus Christ to Judaism and the effects of the grace that has been received through him.

We must now see how the words "And the Word became flesh and dwelt among us" (*kai ho logos sarx egeneto, kai eskenosen en hemin*) relate to the concepts already discussed. It is of course the *logos* of Jewish and Greek thinking which is the subject here, the dynamic, active, rational element that orders the universe and that it is now claimed "is made" *sarx*. The Greek word *sarx* is usually translated "flesh," but unlike "flesh" in English it means "the whole human condition." The Greek *soma*, not used here, means "body" but is, if anything, less than *sarx*. In becoming sarx, the Logos has become one with the "whole human condition" in Jesus. The most difficult word here, in many ways, is *egeneto*, "became" or "was made." It brings with it all the philosophical problems involved in the claim that one thing has become another thing. It certainly does not mean that the Logos ceased to be Logos in becoming *sarx*. Rather, it has to do with the Logos entering into a significant relation with *sarx*. The precise nature of that relation constitutes one of the central questions of classical christology about which there have been centuries of debate. Overall, then, the thrust of the claim in the Prologue is that the Logos' involvement in creation culminates in a specific relation with the human condition in Jesus. The incarnation in Jesus is not the sudden arrival of an otherwise absent Logos, but rather the completion of a process already begun in God's act of creation.

There have, of course, been different interpretations of John 1:10–11. But for the fourth evangelist and his readers, the Logos was by definition active in creation from the beginning, and this is clear in the opening verses of the passage. By following the natural logic of the Logos material in the style adopted here, we can see even more clearly than usual that for the author of John's Prologue, incarnation and creation are thoroughly continuous in the purposes of God.

The Prologue to the Fourth Gospel is a much-loved and frequently read text. But those who emphasize the activity of the Logos in the incarnation at the expense of that in creation do the passage an injustice. The fundamental connection between the incarnation and creation in the overall passage is easier to see if one concentrates on the logic of the Logos material alone. Overall, the Logos is the pre-existent instrument of creation moving in its own realm of creation until its incarnation in Jesus in verse 14. Like wisdom in ancient Israelite thinking, the Logos permeates, orders, and structures the universe. Reading verses 10–11 as referring to the Logos also in creation rather than only in the incarnation underscores the continuity of God's activity, first in creation and then in the incarnation. Instead of taking the emphasis off the incarnation, this reading enables it to be seen in its full perspective in God's overall activity beginning in creation. To tear the incarnation away from creation here, or anywhere, is to do damage to the theology of both, and a notion of the presence of the Logos in the incarnation apart from that in creation is certainly not the intention of the author of the Prologue to the Fourth Gospel. The separation of the incarnation from creation in much modern theology has frequently led to misunderstandings of both. Discussions of christology often omit any mention of God's basic activity in creation, while Christian theological discussions of creation frequently omit any mention of the incarnation. Rereading John's Prologue with the emphases outlined here, however, reminds us just how fundamentally related these two dimensions of God's activity really are.

TWO

BETHLEHEM
WAS JESUS BORN THERE?

"Was Jesus born in Bethlehem?" Most people would probably answer that question with a resounding "Yes, of course he was!" After all, there is evidence in the New Testament, and generations of Christian pilgrims have flocked to Bethlehem to visit his birthplace. But what is the actual historical evidence for Jesus' birth in Bethlehem? A strong tradition runs through the early centuries of Christianity, but before the second century the only evidence we have is the New Testament and it says surprisingly little! Although most Christians take Jesus' birth in Bethlehem for granted, some historians and New Testament scholars have recently come to doubt it, arguing that he was probably really born somewhere else, possibly in Nazareth. The concern in this chapter is with the general question of Jesus' birth in Bethlehem and not with the specific question of the authenticity of the cave in the Church of the Nativity in Bethlehem. In attempting to answer the general question, I first glance briefly at some relevant early Christian literary and archaeological material; second, I consider the New Testament evidence; and third, I focus on the Roman census which in Luke's Gospel takes Mary and Joseph to Bethlehem for Jesus' birth.

Early Christian Literary and Archaeological Material

Outside the New Testament, the tradition of Jesus' birth in Bethlehem first appears in the second century. The Christian apologist Justin Martyr and the author of the apocryphal Gospel the *Protevangelium of James* both knew of Jesus' birth in a cave somewhere in the Bethlehem region. In the third century, the Christian theologian Origen placed the birth inside Bethlehem without mentioning an exact spot. In the fourth century, the emperor Constantine and his mother Helena built a church in Bethlehem focusing on the cave of Jesus' birth. Christian pilgrimage flourished from that time onwards and Christians traveled long distances to pray in the Cave of the Nativity. In the same period, Eusebius, Bishop of Caesarea, affirmed the tradition of Jesus' birth in Bethlehem when he wrote in his *Demonstratio Evangelica* that "all agree that Jesus Christ was born in Bethlehem" (3.2.47). Living in Bethlehem in the late fourth and early fifth century, the Christian scholar Jerome knew a tradition that the site of the birth of Jesus marked by Constantine's church had previously been a shrine dedicated to Venus. "In the cave where once the infant Christ cried," he wrote, "the lover of Venus was lamented" (*Ep*.lviii.3). However, there is insufficient evidence to confirm that the site was used by Christians before that, or to show how or even whether it related to Jesus' birth in the first century. Constantine's church was badly damaged in the sixth century, and the emperor Justinian built another on the same site. Later, in the twelfth century, the Crusaders placed a silver fourteen-pointed star in the cave, bearing the inscription in Latin *Hic de virgine Maria Jesus Christus natus est*—"Here Jesus Christ was born of the Virgin Mary." The church seen in Bethlehem today is largely the Justinian building with Crusader additions. However, although the tradition of Jesus' birth in Bethlehem goes back to the second century, it is the first-century New Testament texts lying behind the tradition which must be the center of any strictly historical investigation into whether or not he was really born there.

The New Testament Evidence

There are no accounts of the birth of Jesus in any New Testament documents apart from the Gospels of Matthew and Luke. Only Romans 1:3 and Galatians 4:4 need be noted as exceptions, but these tell us nothing about Jesus' birth in Bethlehem. This means that the tradition of Jesus' birth in Bethlehem is completely absent from the earliest layers of the New Testament as we now have it.

The only New Testament material relating to Jesus' birth is Matthew 1 and 2, and Luke 1 and 2. The two narratives are familiar, but differ considerably from each other. Jesus is certainly born in Bethlehem in both Matthew and Luke, but that is virtually all the two writers agree about! In order to assess the evidence for Jesus' birth in Bethlehem provided by these two Gospels, it is worth laying out briefly the content of the two narratives noting particularly the role that Bethlehem plays in each.

Matthew begins his infancy narrative with a genealogy (1:1–17). This is followed by an account of the betrothal of Joseph and Mary, the annunciation to Joseph in a dream, and the birth of Jesus in Bethlehem (vv. 18–25). Then, in Matthew 2, we find the wise men (vv. 1–12); the flight to Egypt (vv. 13–15); Herod the Great's massacre of boys under two years old (vv. 16–18); and the return of the family to Israel, and then to Nazareth in Galilee (vv. 19–23).

When we turn to Luke 1 and 2, we find very different material: first, a Prologue (1:1–4); then, an account of the appearance of an angel to Zechariah in the Temple, and the conception of John the Baptist (vv. 5–25); the annunciation to Mary in Nazareth (vv. 26–38); the visitation of Mary to Elizabeth (vv. 39–56); and the birth of John the Baptist (vv. 57–80). In Luke 2, we learn of a census that takes Joseph and Mary from Nazareth to Bethlehem for Jesus' birth (vv. 1–21); the presentation of Jesus in the temple in Jerusalem (vv. 22–40); and finally, the visit to the Jerusalem Temple when Jesus is twelve years old (vv. 41–52).

The role of Bethlehem in the geography of these two narratives is striking. Matthew's account begins in Bethlehem and focuses on Joseph, and there is no mention of Nazareth until 2:23. When the wise men come to visit Jesus, they come into a house in Bethlehem where he has been born. Every impression is given that this is where the family lives, and Joseph, Mary, and Jesus remain there until they depart for Egypt and later Nazareth. By contrast, in Luke, the narrative begins in Nazareth in Galilee where an angel appears to Mary to announce that she will become pregnant. Then, because of a Roman census of the whole world that requires Joseph to travel back to his ancestral hometown, the family makes its way to Bethlehem, because Joseph "was of the house and lineage of David" (Luke 2:4). While the family is in Bethlehem, Jesus is born. They then return to Nazareth where they live. The two narratives, therefore, have a completely different geographical structure: in Matthew, the story moves from Bethlehem to Nazareth, via Egypt, while in Luke it moves from Nazareth to Bethlehem and back again.

On the face of it, the historicity of Jesus' birth in Bethlehem looks pretty solid. In spite of the many differences between Matthew and Luke, Jesus is born in Bethlehem in both narratives. However, it has often been pointed out that Matthew and Luke cannot both be historically correct in all their details: e.g., the family cannot have lived both in Bethlehem and in Nazareth. Although many attempts have been made to harmonize the two accounts, there are always problems. Also, Matthew and Luke's texts both belong to a later layer of the New Testament. Matthew's Gospel is usually thought to have been written about AD 80 and Luke's about AD 90. It is now unclear where the authors got their material from, how far back it goes, and how creative they were at adding and interpreting information. There are, therefore, serious questions concerning the relation of the texts to each other and to the historical events lying behind them. This situation has led some critics, especially perhaps those using a redaction-critical or predominantly literary approach to the Gospels, to conclude that Matthew and Luke are not historically reliable here. But although there are differences and problems, Matthew's and Luke's birth material may be considerably older than their Gospels as we now have them, and there is no need to doubt Jesus' birth in Bethlehem on these grounds alone.

However, there is also other evidence to consider at this point. The silence over Jesus' birth in Bethlehem in the Gospels of Mark and John raises the possibility that he might have been born somewhere else. In Mark 1:9 the author writes, "In those days Jesus came from Nazareth of Galilee," and Bethlehem is not mentioned. The implication here, therefore, could be that Jesus had been born in Nazareth. Later, in Mark 6:1f., Jesus comes into his "own country" or "homeland" (*patrida autou*) and is with his family. Some have taken this to refer to the place where Jesus was born, once again Galilee and possibly Nazareth. Interestingly, the parallels in Matthew 13:53–58 and Luke 4:16–30 (if it is a parallel) and some verses in the Passion Narratives that refer to "Jesus of Nazareth" or "Jesus the Galilean" (cf. Mark 14:67; Matt. 26:69, 71; Luke 22:59) could imply the same thing. It is odd that there is no sign in these later sections of Matthew and Luke that anyone knows of Jesus' birth in Bethlehem. The Fourth Gospel might also appear to support Nazareth as Jesus' birthplace. Lacking any birth in Bethlehem in its opening chapters, the question of the whereabouts of Jesus' birth is raised later in 7:42 with the possible implication that he was born in Galilee rather than Bethlehem. It certainly can appear from all this that the earliest layers of the New Testament material knew of Jesus' birth in Galilee, rather than Bethlehem, and it is easy to see how Matthew and Luke could have added the Bethlehem idea later, failing to harmonize it fully with the older tradition of Jesus' birth in Galilee.

Other possibilities for Jesus' birthplace have also been suggested. For example, in Mark 2:1 the writer says that Jesus entered Capernaum and was "at home" (*en oiko*), perhaps implying that this was his birthplace (cf. Mark 1:9). There is even another Bethlehem in Galilee about seven miles northwest of Nazareth where Jesus might have been born. In this view, Matthew changed this Bethlehem to "Bethlehem of Judea" (2:1) in order to associate

Jesus with David. Where Nazareth is not specifically mentioned, of course, the suggestion of Galilee could leave the birth of Jesus almost anywhere in the region.

By this stage, however, hypotheses seem to grow wild and we must draw back. Although many problems remain, it is clearly possible to read Mark 1:9 and 6:1, and the other texts mentioned, as presupposing Jesus' birth in Bethlehem. Mark 1:9 does not necessarily imply that Jesus was born in Nazareth, and 6:1 can refer to Jesus' home at the time of his ministry and not to his birthplace. One's home and one's birthplace are not necessarily the same place. As for Mark 2:1, it is not at all necessary to assume that "at home" here means Jesus' birthplace. The idea that Jesus was born in Bethlehem in Galilee cannot be substantiated, and finally, even though John 7:42 is an important text, it is riddled with irony and cannot form the basis of any strictly historical reconstruction. In any case, the irony there probably implies that Jesus was actually born in Bethlehem! Basically, none of the texts frequently cited as pointing away from Bethlehem as Jesus' birthplace necessarily do so. None of the other suggested possibilities seriously affect the view that Jesus was born in Bethlehem and they are all, in fact, compatible with his having been born there. It is also important to remember, once again, that Matthew and Luke may well be working with traditions and material that predate their Gospels and go back much further than is often thought. Much more serious a stumbling block in the basic task here is the question of the Roman census referred to in Luke 2:2.

The Roman Census in Luke

At the beginning of his chapter on the birth of Jesus, Luke writes that, "In those days a decree went out from Caesar Augustus that all the world should be enrolled. This was the first enrollment, when Quirinius was governor of Syria" (2:1f.; cf. Acts 5:36–37). In 1:5 Luke has already made the point that John the Baptist's birth took place "in the days of Herod, King of Judea," and in this he agrees with Matthew 2:1. Jesus' birth date, confused by later miscalculations in the sixth century, is generally now reckoned to have been around 6–4 BCE, and in Luke's scheme it is in the same period as John's birth. However, it is often pointed out that Jesus cannot have been born both during the reign of Herod the Great and when Quirinius was governor of Syria, which we know to have been in CE 6–7. Overall, there are serious questions here concerning whether there ever was a census at the time of Herod the Great, and whether Quirinius was ever governor of Syria during Herod's time. I shall consider these two basic problems in turn.

First, the census. There has been widespread skepticism concerning the occurrence of a census during the reign of Herod the Great. New Testament scholars often claim that there is no evidence in Roman history of a census of the whole world during Herod's time, and that the Roman censuses we do know of did not require people to travel to their ancestral hometowns or to take their families with them.

Second, Quirinius. We know quite a lot about Publius Sulpicius Quirinius from the writers Josephus, Tacitus, and Strabo. Quirinius was indeed governor of Syria, but not at the time of Jesus' birth. When Herod the Great died in c. 4 BCE, his son Archelaeus succeeded him in Judea but fell from power in CE 6–7 when a Roman prefect was installed. Judea was annexed to the province of Syria, and Quirinius, who was governor of Syria, instigated a census. But this was in CE 6–7, not 6–4 BCE when Jesus was born. Josephus mentions this census and comments that it was the first of its kind to occur. In the second century, the Christian writer Tertullian refers to some censuses at the time of Saturninus who was governor of Syria in 9–6 BCE. Some have suggested that Luke might have been thinking of him, but there is insufficient reason for linking Luke's census with those of Saturninus. Indeed, Raymond Brown, in his *The Birth of the Messiah,* concludes that "there is no serious reason to believe that there was a Roman census of Palestine under Quirinius during the reign of Herod the Great" (p. 554).

All this has led to a negative view of Luke as a historian, and a popular view has been that Luke was more interested in theology than history. Although he has given Jesus' birth a setting on the stage of world history, commentators often conclude that Luke's real interest is in the Davidic symbolism of Bethlehem: it was the place of David's birth and anointing (1 Sam. 16); he himself had called a census (2 Sam. 24; cf. Ps. 87:6); and it was the town from which a significant leader of Israel would eventually arise (Micah 5:2). On this view, Luke was simply using the census as a scene-change mechanism in his dramatic presentation of Jesus as a messianic figure. But of course, if there was no census, Jesus' birth in Bethlehem is cast in doubt.

However, there have been other, more optimistic assessments of Luke as a historian. At the end of the nineteenth century, W.M. Ramsay published a work titled *Was Christ Born at Bethlehem?* He claimed that Luke was referring not to a single census of the "whole world," but to one of a series of local censuses that had parallels in Egypt and Syria. Ramsay maintained that a census could have had several installments beginning in the time of Herod the Great and finishing in CE 6–7 when Quirinius was indeed governor of Syria. Ramsay also claimed, on the basis of two marble inscriptions, that Quirinius could have been governor of Syria twice. It is certainly striking that the Greek word used by Luke for governor (*hegemon*) can have a breadth of meaning from any general "leader" up to the specific leadership of the emperor. Ramsay argued that Quirinius acted on behalf of the emperor for Syria around the time of Jesus' birth and could rightly have been called *hegemon*.

All this begins to make more sense of Luke's comment that "this was the first enrollment," and that Jesus was born "when Quirinius was governor of Syria." However, it cannot be proven that Ramsay's periodic censuses ever took place in Judea, and his inscriptions are actually more ambiguous than he admits. Nevertheless, his book drew attention to the complexity of the historical issues and to the possibility that Luke might be much more reliable than is often claimed.

In the 1960s, A. N. Sherwin-White took a similarly optimistic view of Luke, as did I. Howard Marshall later when he wrote that "the character of the census described by Luke is far from impossible" (p. 102).

Overall, the historical evidence for a census at the time of Jesus' birth is inconclusive. But although Luke's comments are open to radically different interpretations, it is not wise to dismiss him too quickly as a reliable source of historical evidence. If Luke's census is historical, the case for Jesus' birth in Bethlehem might be strengthened, although many problems would remain. On the other hand, if Luke's census is not historical, Matthew's account becomes the only New Testament source of evidence, and its historical reliability can also easily be questioned. However, even though Matthew obviously has theological interests in Bethlehem, his material could still contain historical fact, and Bethlehem is where the story begins in his account. In the end, both Matthew and Luke thought it important enough to place Jesus' birth in Bethlehem, and in principle the tradition could stretch back well behind the Gospels as we now have them.

The quest for the historicity of Jesus' birth in Bethlehem is a fascinating, if sometimes frustrating maze of problems and questions. In weighing and interpreting the evidence one confronts both history and theology, and a definite overall answer is tantalizingly elusive. It is clear that there is a strong tradition of Jesus' birth in Bethlehem in the early Christian centuries, and there is no evidence that anyone objected to this on historical grounds at the time. But it is also clear that the New Testament evidence that lies behind the later tradition is weaker than is sometimes realized. Some New Testament scholars have concluded that Jesus was born in Galilee, but the texts cited in support of this view can equally well be read presupposing Bethlehem. Theological symbolism and historicity are not mutually exclusive, and the historicity of Jesus' birth in Bethlehem cannot be dismissed on the grounds that it is a Davidic symbol. Bethlehem is, after all, the only place specifically mentioned in the New Testament as Jesus' birthplace, and the Gospels of Matthew and Luke may contain traditions that go back to his lifetime. In the end, even though we cannot know definitely that Jesus was born in Bethlehem, it is not incompatible with the evidence, and therefore not unreasonable to conclude that the tradition could easily have some basis in historical fact.

THREE

MORE THAN A PROPHET?

JESUS AMONG THE PROPHETS OF ANCIENT ISRAEL

Christian believers and theologians don't often think of Jesus as a Prophet. They usually think of him primarily as "Lord," "Son of God," "Son of Man," or in terms of one of the other New Testament or traditional christological titles or expressions. "Surely Jesus is more than just a prophet like Amos or Isaiah," many would say, and begin to look elsewhere for words to capture his full significance.

But the word "prophet" carries powerful overtones from Israel's history and is, after all, used of Jesus a number of times in the New Testament. It is therefore a term that should feature more often in discussions of the significance of Jesus. Basically, the prophet in ancient Israel was the one who "spoke out" the will of God into situations of religious and social injustice and also "acted out," often in symbolic ways, the will of God for his people. Even though the word "prophet" is not the most important title for Jesus in the New Testament, it is something of a neglected element in the New Testament tradition and has lost any central place in contemporary Christian reflection about Jesus. There is much to be recovered about Jesus' significance from looking at him in the light of this background. There are, of course, other more important words for Jesus in the New Testament; he is certainly "more than a prophet" in the Gospels; and the word doesn't adequately capture his full identity. But a great deal can still be learned by thinking of him as one who "spoke out" the word of God in his own particular situation and who acted it out unto death in his public ministry.

In this chapter, I first consider the nature of the prophets of ancient Israel; and second, I survey the New Testament material relating to Jesus as a prophet. Seeing Jesus among the prophets of ancient Israel enables an important aspect of his identity to emerge: he revealed God's will to his people in word and deed.

Prophecy in Ancient Israel

What were the defining characteristics of the prophets of ancient Israel? Most people are aware of the names of some of the prophets: Abraham and Moses; Miriam and Deborah; Elijah and Elisha; and the long line of prophets from Amos and Hosea, through Isaiah and Micah, to Jeremiah and Ezekiel and beyond. But what were they actually like and what did they really do?

The prophetic tradition in Israel is usually divided into three historical periods: pre-classical; classical; and exilic and post-exilic. There are differences and similarities between the basic types, and post-exilic prophecy differs significantly from pre-exilic. The quickest way to appreciate something of what the basic prophetic types were in ancient Israel is by way of etymology. Behind the English word "prophet" lies the Greek *prophetes* meaning either "to speak forth" or "to speak before," i.e., before an event. It translates three different Hebrew words in the Hebrew Bible: (1) *navi*: this is the word that is translated most frequently as *prophetes* in the Septuagint. It probably stems from an Akkadian verb *nabu* meaning "to call," "to announce," or "to name." It can also mean "one who calls" and "one who is called." In Genesis 20:7 Abraham is called a *navi*; in Deuteronomy 18:15, the prophet who will be raised up is a *navi*; (2) *hozeh*: this word means "a visionary" and clearly refers to the experience that gives rise to the particular revelations the person receives. The word is used, for example, of Gad in 1 Chronicles 21:9; and (3) *ro'eh*: this means "one who sees" or "a seer." In 1 Samuel 9:9, Samuel is called a *ro'eh*. In 1 Chronicles 29:29 Samuel, Nathan, and Gad are named as *ro'eh, navi*, and *hozeh* together. In 1 Samuel 9:9 we learn that "he who is now called *navi* was formerly called *ro'eh*." Although these words had different emphases, the range of meaning was very broad indeed and eventually they came to overlap.

In addition to these three main words, we should also note the Hebrew expressions *ish ha-Elohim* or "man of God," and *benei ha-nevi'im* or "sons of the prophets." Both expressions occur in the Elijah and Elisha narratives in 1 Kings 17–2 Kings 13. Elijah and Elisha are associated with divine power and symbolic actions. The "sons of the prophets," often associated with music and ecstasy, are a group of prophets or a prophetic guild, although the problem of their real identity is complex. Overall, the basic thrust in the meaning of the main words *navi*, *hozeh*, and *ro'eh* certainly has to do with "speaking out," announcing, and naming, and with a particular discernment of God's will on the part of the ones called.

Because of the wide range of meaning found in the various words used in association with the prophets in the Hebrew Bible, it is notoriously difficult to find a single characteristic of the prophet. Yet we can note some basic features from prophetic literature. The prophets are appointed to "speak out" and often use the words "Thus says the Lord." The texts that tell of the calling of the prophets indicate foundational events in their ministries; they are inaugurations, sendings out, or re-dedications. They are occasions of revelation and inspiration when God communicates his word to the prophet and prompts the prophet to speak. Amos, for example, tells Amaziah the priest of Bethel how he received his summons from God: "I am no prophet, nor a prophet's son; but I am a herdsman, and a dresser of sycamore trees, and the LORD took me from following the flock, and the LORD said to me 'Go, prophesy to my people Israel'" (Amos 7:14–15). Other obvious examples are the calls of Isaiah, Ezekiel, Zechariah, and Jeremiah. Key characteristics of the prophet, then, are "speaking out," a specific calling, divine inspiration, and specific revelation from God.

Speaking out the word of God was not just a matter of delivering a message, however. The prophetic utterance was itself a creative act that could bring about a radical change in the circumstances into which it was spoken. The utterance of the word (*dabar*) had a creative and dynamic effect on those who heard it. Indeed, God's word which was spoken by the prophets was the same word which was active in creation (Ps. 33:6). But the speaking of the word of God by the prophets has been perceived in a variety of different ways. Was the word spoken primarily into the contemporary situation of the prophet? Or was it a message for, or indeed about, the future?

The notion of the prophets as figures who predicted future events came to a head in the Second Temple period, and later, and was developed, for example, by early Christians who saw Jewish prophetic texts fulfilled in Jesus. By the time of the Second Temple period and of early Christianity, the prophets of old were, of course, essentially texts rather than people, and the notion of prediction of future events was read back into them. This notion of the prophets developed in a number of subsequent places, not least in Rabbinic Judaism and in modern Zionism. But it is clear that in their own day, the focus of the prophetic voice in ancient Israel was on their own contemporary circumstances, and not on the distant future. Insofar as there was any future prediction, it was the imminent future that was in view. As has been frequently claimed, the prophet was a "*forth*teller rather than a *fore*teller." He or she spoke the word of God into the contemporary situation, usually one of social and religious injustice.

The prophets of ancient Israel did not only speak God's word to the people; they also spoke the people's word to God; they were intercessors on behalf of the people. In Jeremiah 15:1, for example, Moses and Samuel are seen as intercessors. The notion of the prophet as "intercessor" is fundamental to the prophetic identity in ancient Israel. The traffic of language between God and the prophets flowed, as it were, in both directions.

However, the role of the prophet in ancient Israel was not only one of "speaking out" the word of God into the contemporary situation. It was also a physical, bodily, and practical matter. That is to say, words were intertwined with deeds, and speech with action. Israel's prophetic literature is heavy with wonder-working, symbolic actions, and physical involvement in social and political issues: Zedekiah famously makes himself horns of iron (1 Kings 22); Elijah and Elisha heal the sons of the widow of Zarephath (1 Kings 17) and of the Shunammite woman (2 Kings 4); Hosea gets married (Hos. 1:2–9; 3:1–3); children of the prophets have symbolic names (Is. 7); Maher-shalal-Hash-baz is written on a stone (Is. 8). More specifically, Isaiah goes "naked and barefoot" in Jerusalem (Is. 20); Jeremiah smashes a pot (Jer. 19); carries a yoke on his back (Jer. 27) which is broken; buys a field in Anathoth (Jer. 32); and buries stones in the ground in Egypt (Jer. 43). Ezekiel performs more symbolic actions than any of the other Israelite prophets: he sketches the siege of Jerusalem on a brick (4:1); lies paralyzed on his side for 390 days (4:4ff.); eats small amounts of bread and unclean food (4:9ff.); and shaves his head (5:1). These and other such acts are the practical working out of the uttering of the word of God to the people. They are the physical, bodily, social aspect of the message worked out in the face of injustice and conflict and as such are part of the prophecy itself.

This brief overview of some of the characteristics of the prophets in ancient Israel shows that although prophecy was a complex and multifaceted phenomenon, two elements are abundantly clear: (1) that the prophet was called to "speak out," "announce," or "name" God's will directly into the contemporary situation; and (2) that the "speaking out" involved some sort of symbolic physical action on the social and political scene in which the prophet lived. Prophecy was a matter, not only of speaking, but also of acting; it involved deeds as well as words. In fact, the symbolic actions legitimized the speaking and enacted the message, and both clearly formed a fundamental part of delivering God's message to his people. The prophet revealed God's will in word and deed. The message was for the prophets' own times rather than for the future. With these characteristics of the prophet in mind, we can now turn to the New Testament to see to what extent Jesus is portrayed in these terms.

Jesus the Prophet

Any consideration of Jesus as a prophet must take into account his place within the Judaism of his day. One of the assured results of the third quest for the historical Jesus is that he was indeed a Jewish teacher and preacher of his time and should be seen primarily within the context of Second Temple Judaism. But what sort of a prophet was he within that context, and did he bear any of the characteristics of the prophets of ancient Israel? Many recent writers have portrayed Jesus as an apocalyptic prophet of some sort, announcing the coming of the end-time. Others have rejected such a view with equal vehemence. The U.S. New Testament scholar Ben Witherington III has recently portrayed Jesus as a sage, a seer, and a prophet. The New Testament writers are certainly interested in prophecy and the prophets of ancient Israel, but their notion of prophecy was largely one of prediction: the ancient prophets predicted events that later came to pass in the life, death, and resurrection of Jesus. Matthew's "fulfillment quotations" are the most obvious example of this. From this angle, Jesus is not so much a prophet as a fulfiller of prophecies, and although he is clearly aligned with the prophets of Israel in the Gospels, it is not always clear what sort of a prophet they saw him as. Although he is a prophet in the New Testament, he is clearly also "more than a prophet": he fulfills prophecy. Even so, he is called a prophet and clearly "speaks out" and reveals God's will in word and deed.

To what extent, then, is Jesus portrayed as a prophet by the New Testament writers? Once again, approaching the subject by way of etymology will shed some light here. In the New Testament, the Greek noun *prophetes* is made up of *pro* meaning "before" and *phe* meaning "speak." The basic meaning of "prophet," therefore, can be "one who speaks before" or "one who speaks forth," or "one who proclaims." The ambiguity in the word provokes different emphases in interpretation here, with the notion of "speaking before" or "predicting" often prevailing. In the Greek world the word already had a wide variety of general meanings and uses. Poets and philosophers, for example, were called prophets. For Plato, religious or divine inspiration was similar to that experienced by poets, and the word could be used of anyone so influenced. It was used frequently to interpret the communications of gods to humanity, but could also be used of less lofty matters, for example, of the person making the announcements at the annual games! It is clear, then, that "speaking out" was the dominant sense of the word "prophet" in the Greek world.

In the New Testament Gospels the noun *prophetes* occurs frequently. It is used 37 times in Matthew; 6 times in Mark; 29 times in Luke; 30 times in Acts; and 14 times in John, although these are not all in relation to Jesus. The word is mostly used of John the Baptist and of some of the prophets of ancient Israel who are mentioned by name. In fact, the word *prophetes* occurs quite rarely in relation to Jesus himself. In "Q," one of the oldest layers of the Gospel tradition, Jesus is never called a prophet. In Mark 6:15 and 8:28 he is associated with the prophets of Israel. Mark doesn't explicitly call him a prophet there, although in 6:4 he is presented as standing in line with the prophets, albeit implicitly rather than explicitly. However, even if Mark does intend Jesus to be understood as a prophet, it is not an idea he develops in the rest of his Gospel except perhaps by implication as Jesus "speaks out" generally. Similarly, Matthew has few specific references to Jesus as a prophet. In Matthew 16:14, at Caesarea Philippi, he follows Mark but with the added reference to Jeremiah; in the Passion Narrative at Matthew 26:68 the false witnesses say "Prophesy to us, you Christ!" Perhaps the most significant text in Matthew, however, is 21:11, where at the entry into Jerusalem the crowds say of Jesus, "This is the prophet Jesus from Nazareth of Galilee." He then enters the city and the Temple, and the action in the Temple follows. In addition to the specific uses of the word *prophetes* in Matthew, there are also more general senses in which Matthew might be seen to portray Jesus as a prophet, for example, in his presentation of Jesus as a "New Moses" or in his connection of Jesus to Isaiah's suffering servant.

It is Luke among the synoptic evangelists who is most interested in portraying Jesus as a prophet and who links him with the prophets of ancient Israel. In Luke 4:24 in the synagogue in Nazareth (the parallel to Mark 6:4) Luke aligns Jesus with the prophets and specifically with the rejection of the prophets; in 7:16, after raising the Widow of Nain's son, the crowd says, "A great prophet has arisen among us"; and in 24:19 on the Road to Emmaus the two travelers identify Jesus as a prophet. Luke uses the prophet motif to stress the rejection of Jesus, and his coming death, the fate of the prophet to die in Jerusalem (11:45–52; 13:31–35; cf. 6:22–23). In the Fourth Gospel, there are four occasions when Jesus is specifically called a prophet: in 4:19 with the woman at the well in Samaria; in 6:14 after the feeding of the five thousand; in 7:40 at the feast of Tabernacles in Jerusalem; and in 9:17 with the man born blind. The meanings and overtones in these passages vary and the emphases in each case are different, although overall Jesus is clearly associated with the prophets of ancient Israel. It is also in the Fourth Gospel that reference is made to "that prophet" of Deuteronomy 18:15. Clearly it was expected that a prophet would be raised up on the last day (cf. 1 Macc. 4:46; 14:41; 4 Ezra 2:18). The question in John 1:21 is whether John the Baptist is that prophet. The answer is "no." The implication here could conceivably be that Jesus *is* that prophet, as he certainly is in Acts 7:37.

In considering the extent to which Jesus is portrayed as a prophet in the New Testament, however, it is not enough to look only at texts where the actual word "prophet" occurs. Some of Jesus' sayings in the Gospels can be seen to be prophetic in style and/or content, for example: (1) the words "Verily I say to you" have been seen by some as a parallel to the prophetic "Thus says the Lord," although there is no evidence that Jesus saw his words as the actual words of God in these contexts, as the prophets of ancient Israel seem to have done when they used their expression; (2) "Who among you?" is used in the context of Jesus' parables and might be seen to have prophetic parallels (Is. 42:23; 50:1; cf. Hag. 2:3), although they are few; (3) the two-part structure of some of Jesus' sayings indicates a present/future distinction, e.g., Mark 8:35, "whoever would save his life will lose it . . ."; and (4) the predictions that Jesus makes, e.g., about the coming of the kingdom of God, the Son of Man, his own death, the destruction of Jerusalem and the Temple, and the apocalyptic material in Mark 13 *et par.*, might all be seen to indicate that Jesus was an eschatological or apocalyptic prophet of some sort. Establishing the authenticity of Jesus' sayings here, of course, can be a very difficult matter, but although we may not be able to build up our picture of Jesus the prophet on the basis of such sayings, they can, nevertheless, be seen to be in line with his having been a prophet, or at least with the Gospel writers presenting him as such.

Perhaps the general picture of Jesus as a prophet in the Gospels is as important in all this as the use of the word "prophet" or the sayings material. For example, parallels have been noted between Jesus' baptism and the coming of the spirit upon him, and the classical prophetic "call" already noted; and between Jesus' vision of Satan falling from heaven (Luke 10:18), and the Israelite prophetic visions; and between Jesus' suffering and death in Jerusalem, and the same theme in the prophetic material. Over half a century ago now, C. H. Dodd suggested fifteen basic prophetic elements that feature in the narratives of Jesus' life in the Gospels. They were:

- the authority of his teaching;
- the poetic character of some of his sayings;
- visions and auditions;
- predictions;
- symbolic actions;
- a vital form of religion as opposed to the cult;
- a link with apocalyptic;
- announcing the reign of God;
- preaching repentance;
- being conscious of a special calling;
- receiving divine revelation;
- following God;
- being conscious of a mission to Israel;
- expecting something to happen as a result of his death; and
- showing prophetic piety.

Whether or not these are all individually specifically prophetic elements is debatable, but in any case the most important among them are: (1) Jesus' announcement of the kingdom of God; (2) his teaching with authority; and (3) his symbolic actions. In Mark 1:15, Jesus announces the kingdom or reign of God; then in 1:22 the reader learns that the people in Capernaum "were astonished at his teaching, for he taught them as one who had authority." The Greek word *exousia* here, usually translated "authority," clearly indicates divine authority, and although the word is not specifically associated with the prophets of ancient Israel, it captures the same sense as the classical prophetic "Thus says the Lord." It is striking, furthermore, that the voice of authority in Mark 1:22 is followed by the healing of a man with an unclean spirit. Thereafter, Jesus' teaching, for example in parables, is intertwined with his "works of mighty power." It is here, in Jesus' authoritative teaching and speaking, closely related to his physical actions (like so many of the prophets before him), that a specifically prophetic element can be seen.

In the Gospels, Jesus' symbolic actions seem evident enough. In the synoptics, he performs "works of mighty power" (*dunameis*) and in the Fourth Gospel, signs (*semeia*). Some of these might be seen as parallels to some of the Israelite prophets' wonder-working or symbolic actions: e.g., sending out the twelve; giving symbolic names to some of them; the feeding stories; the healing stories; walking on water; and, not least, the entry into Jerusalem and the action in the Temple. Not all commentators are happy to think of such actions as strictly prophetic, but some of the actions seem pretty close, especially, for example, Jesus' action in the Temple which is linked up with specific teaching. Overall, it is clear that there is evidence in the New Testament that Jesus is seen as standing in line with the prophets of ancient Israel even though he is clearly also greater than them. He speaks out the will of God in announcing the coming kingdom of God, and performs symbolic actions that enact the message to the people. More specifically, he reveals the will of God in both word and deed.

In the popular understanding of Jesus, many titles and expressions from the New Testament and elsewhere are used to try to clinch his identity. The idea that he was a "prophet," however, is not widely explored. In the New Testament, it is clear that Jesus is at least associated with the prophets of ancient Israel. Indeed, it seems fair to say that he is presented as a prophet even though he is, strictly speaking, "more than a prophet." The prophets of ancient Israel were men and women who were inspired leaders in their communities; who "spoke out" in difficult social and political circumstances; and who "acted out" the will of God for the people in symbolic actions. Rather than predicting the future, they spoke God's will into their own situations and often died for it. Several different words in the Hebrew Bible are translated as "prophet," but it is clear that the overall significance of these men and women lies in their "speaking out" and "acting out." They were inspired individuals who revealed the will of God to the people.

In the same way, Jesus is portrayed in the New Testament as one who announced the coming kingdom of God; taught with authority; performed symbolic actions; and was put to death. Even though there may be distinctions between the prophets of Israel and Jesus, he stands in line with them in that he was moved by the spirit, "spoke out" with authority into the circumstances of his time, and acted out his message in particular deeds revealing the will of God to the people. It is especially in the speaking and acting together that the prophetic identity can be seen, and like the prophets of ancient Israel, Jesus revealed God's will in word and deed, in and for his community, often in the face of difficulty and opposition. In the end he, like many of them, died in Jerusalem as a result. The combination of speaking and acting "unto death" catches the nature of the prophetic spirit, and even though strictly speaking Jesus was "more than a prophet," the recovery of his prophetic dimension is an important step in establishing who he was.

FOUR

SON OF GOD AND SON OF MAN

CLEARING UP SOME MISUNDERSTANDINGS

The idea that Jesus is the "Son of God" is extremely powerful in contemporary popular Christianity. Acceptance of this expression is usually taken to mean belief in Jesus' divinity and in the traditional "two natures" christology of Chalcedon drawn up in CE 451. Agreement that Jesus is or was the "Son of God" is taken as an affirmation that he was indeed God incarnate, the second person of the trinity made flesh. Denial that Jesus is or was the "Son of God" is, therefore, obviously taken as a denial of the traditional doctrine of the incarnation and the whole system of Christian belief that goes with it.

Even though this understanding of "Son of God" has firm foundations in the Christian tradition, it is actually not what the expression originally meant in ancient Judaism and not what it means in the writings of the New Testament. The partner expression "Son of Man" is used frequently of Jesus in the Gospels, although one hears it less in contemporary Christian usage. When it does occur today it is usually taken to refer to Jesus' humanity in contrast to his divinity.

This polarization of meaning in the two expressions is somewhat naïve when one considers their respective histories, although it does reflect more or less how many of the church fathers understood the expressions. This chapter considers the meanings of "Son of God" and "Son of Man" in the New Testament and attempts to show that each has a complex background and is used in different ways by different writers. There are many issues surrounding the interpretation of these two expressions, especially "Son of Man," but it is clear that each meant something rather different from what it came to mean subsequently and what it often means when it is used today. So let us consider each expression in turn.

Son of God

A consideration of the expression "Son of God" as used of Jesus in the New Testament immediately raises a number of other related questions. Sonship language is, of course, metaphorical and implies "father." Once we ask what is meant by calling Jesus "Son of God" we are immediately faced with questions of his understanding of God as father, his relationship with God, and the wider question of his own consciousness of being God's son. The concern in this section, however, is with how the expression "Son of God" is used of Jesus in the New Testament rather than with the wider questions about his status as son. Before turning to the New Testament use, however, let us first consider the background of "son of god" in the Greco-Roman world and in the world of ancient Judaism.

In the Greco-Roman world, the expression "son of god" was used very widely of a number of different people. In the Greek myths, a number of figures were thought of as "sons of god"; for example, Zeus was known as the father of all men, so that all men were his sons. Famous Greek philosophers and rulers of ancient Egypt were also "sons of god," as was Augustus Caesar in the Roman world. In ancient Judaism, the expression was used equally widely. All male Jews were in principle "sons of God," and the concept of sonship and the actual expression "son(s) of god" were used frequently. The idea and expression could be used of individual Israelites or of the whole of Israel (e.g., Ex. 4:22–23; Deut. 14:1; 32:8, 19; 1 Chron. 17:13; Is. 43:6; Jer. 31:9, 20; Hosea 1:10; 11:1). It was also used of particular people such as charismatics, righteous men, and those who suffered (e.g., Wisd. 2:13, 16, 18; 5:5; Sirach 4:10); of the King of Israel himself (e.g., 2 Sam. 7:14; Ps. 2:7; 89:27–29; Is. 9:6–7); and of heavenly creatures such as angels (e.g., Gen. 6:1–4; Job 1:6; 2:1; 38:7; Ps. 29:1; 82:1, 6; 89:6–8). Thus, although "son(s) of God" did refer to a special relationship with God, it was used very widely and could be used of everybody from ordinary people to those in specific roles. The common element was that the "sons" belonged to God's entourage, whether on earth or in heaven.

In the New Testament, Jesus is referred to frequently as God's son, in addition to the actual expression "Son of God" being used of him. Where the expression itself occurs, there are a variety of emphases among the different writers. Paul often calls Jesus God's son, especially in Romans 1–8 and in Galatians (e.g., Rom. 8:29, 32; Gal. 1:16; 4:4ff.), and also uses sonship language generally of Christian believers (e.g., Rom. 8:14, 23). There is no doubt that he and other early Christians in the first years after Jesus' death and resurrection thought of Jesus as God's son. However, Paul actually only uses the expression "Son of God" of Jesus three times (Rom. 1:4; 2 Cor. 1:19; Gal. 2:20). The earliest layers of the New Testament, including the letters of Paul, use the expression "Son of God" specifically in relation to Jesus' resurrection and exaltation. At Romans 1:4, Jesus is "designated Son of God" by his resurrection. The same emphasis can be found in Acts, for example at 13:33 where God's promise is fulfilled by raising Jesus (cf. 9:20) and where Psalm 2:7 is quoted in support: "You are my Son, today I have begotten you." Psalm 2 was probably originally used of the inauguration of the King of Israel and is used here to mark the inauguration of Jesus as God's son (cf. Heb. 1:5; 5:5).

In the Gospel of Mark, the notion that Jesus is "Son of God" is particularly associated with his death (15:39), but it is also used more broadly. Mark uses "Son of God" in the opening verse of his Gospel (1:1), although it is absent in some manuscripts. He also uses it in relation to Jesus' baptism (1:11), providing a strong echo of Psalm 2:7 and marking the beginning of Jesus' ministry. Interestingly, it is the demons in Mark who recognize Jesus as Son of God early on in the Gospel (3:11; 5:7), and sonship language appears periodically thereafter (9:7; 12:6; 13:32; 14:61). In all, in Mark it is clear that Jesus' sonship is established at his baptism, but it is played out in his ministry as he makes his way to the cross. Matthew basically follows Mark's uses of the expression "Son of God," although he also uses it on a number of significant new occasions (4:3, 6; 14:33; 16:16; 27:40, 43). Sonship language is already used of Jesus in the infancy narrative (2:15; cf. Hosea 11:1), and Matthew effectively sees Jesus' sonship as inaugurated at his conception. For Luke, the use of "Son of God" is somewhat less important (see 1:35; 3:38; 4:3, 9, 41; 22:70). He takes the expression from the tradition in Mark and merges it in with other titles for Jesus. Even so, as in Matthew, Jesus' sonship is inaugurated at his conception, and there is no doubt that he is "Son of God" for Luke.

Although "Son of God" is important in the synoptic Gospels, it is even more significant in the Fourth Gospel and in the Epistle to the Hebrews. In the Fourth Gospel, of course, the climate is quite different from that in the synoptics. The expression "Son of God" and the language of Jesus as "son" occur frequently. While Christians are called children (*tekna*) in the Johannine epistles, "son" (*huios*) is reserved for Jesus in the Gospel (e.g., 1:34, 49; 3:18, 36; 11:27; 19:7; 20:31). The son is personally related to the Father (3:35; 5:20; 10:17; 17:23–26); the Father sends the son (3:17; 4:34; 5:23, 30, 37; 6:38, 44; 10:36; 17:18) and gives everything to him (3:35; 5:22, 26); the son does what the Father does (5:19–21); the Father and the son are one (10:30; 14:7), but the Father is also greater than the son (14:28); believing in the son is central (3:17–18); and the son is the source of eternal life (3:16, 36; 5:21; 6:40). The key difference in John is that the notion of pre-existence in the Prologue permeates everything that is said of Jesus the son (e.g., 17:5, 24). His status as son is a permanent or eternal status which is not inaugurated at his resurrection, baptism, or conception. He is the "only-begotten son" from the beginning (1:14, 18; 3:16, 18). In the Fourth Gospel, then, there is a strong sense that Jesus is one with God in his status as Son of God. But he is also clearly distinct from him (1:1). The notion of Jesus' sonship is also important in 1 John (4:9–5:20). In the epistle to the Hebrews, Jesus' status as son is related throughout to his suffering and death, which are so central to the theology of Hebrews. Jesus the son is the one through whom God has spoken (1:2); as in the Fourth Gospel, the son is the one through whom God has created the world (1:2); he "reflects the glory and bears the very stamp of God's nature" (1:3); and he is higher than the angels (1:4–13). Jesus' sonship is related to his status as High Priest (4:14–5:10 [where the writer quotes Ps. 2:7]; 7:3, 28), and he is made perfect through suffering (2:10; 5:9; 7:28). The overall sense here is that Jesus does have a pre-existent divine sonship, but it is thoroughly related to his life of suffering and his death.

In short, the expression "Son of God" could be used of any suitably qualified person in the ancient Greco-Roman and Jewish worlds. In the New Testament it evokes Jesus' special relationship with God in a number of different ways. Mark focuses on Jesus' death as the key element of his sonship, while Matthew and Luke see his baptism or conception as establishing it. In the Fourth Gospel and Hebrews, sonship is associated with Jesus' pre-existence. However, although "Son of God" does indicate a special relationship between Jesus and God, it clearly doesn't yet indicate "the divinity of Christ" as it came to do in the christological statements of the later councils of the church and as it often does in contemporary usage.

Son of Man

When we turn to the expression "Son of Man" in the New Testament, the situation is much more complex. It is well known that, apart from one reference in Acts (7:56) and two in the Book of Revelation (1:13; 14:14), the expression "the Son of Man" is found in the New Testament only in the Gospels, and almost entirely on the lips of Jesus. Furthermore, the use in the New Testament is unique because the expression is preceded by the definite article: "*the* Son of Man." One of the many mysteries of this phrase concerns when the definite article was added and when the expression became a title. This section surveys the background and use of this expression in the New Testament in order to clarify what the phrase might have meant to anyone using, hearing, or reading it in the first century CE. The background will take us into key texts in the Hebrew Bible and other Jewish literature of the period. The New Testament survey will take us through the uses of this expression by the evangelists and the key scholarly views concerning its meaning.

What, then, might the expression "the Son of Man" have meant to the writers of the Gospels? What was its meaning in the Judaism of the first century CE? In Hebrew poetry it is used simply as a parallel for "man," and the words are *ben Adam*. A good example is Psalm 8:4: "what is man that thou art mindful of him, and the son of man that thou dost care for him?" (e.g., Ps. 80:17). This verse constitutes a case of Hebrew poetic parallelism known as *parallelismus membrorum*. The expression occurs in the second half of the verse and means what the basic word in the first half means, i.e., simply "man." The expression also occurs about a hundred times in the Book of Ezekiel where the prophet is himself referred to as "son of man" (e.g., 2:1, 3, 8; 3:1, 4; 4:1; 5:1). Again the Hebrew is *ben Adam* and the meaning is simply "man." A significant occurrence, however, is in Daniel 7:13 where the setting is apocalyptic. There, in a night vision, four beasts come up out of the sea and the Ancient of Days or God takes his seat. Then "one like a son of man" comes to the Ancient of Days (7:13). This section of the Book of Daniel (2:4–7:28) is written in Aramaic, not Hebrew, and the expression here is *bar enash* which means simply "son of man," that is "one in human form." The expression lacks the definite article here and is not a technical term or title. The son of man is a human figure, although he is now in the heavenly court being presented to God. He is given dominion, glory, and kingdom (7:14) and clearly represents Israel in some way, perhaps the whole nation or simply a remnant. In any case, he is a figure associated with suffering and vindication; a human figure in the heavenly court.

The expression "son of man" is also found in three other significant texts: (1) the Book of Enoch; (2) 2 Esdras or 4 Ezra; and (3) the Dead Sea Scrolls. In the Book of Enoch, the expression occurs in chapters 37–71 (46:1, 2, 3, 4; 48:2; 62:5, 7, 9, 14; 63:11; 69:26, 27; 70:1; 71:14). The date of these chapters is problematic and the text is not all of one piece. It probably comes from sometime during the period of the first century BCE–first century CE. Other chapters of Enoch were discovered at Qumran but these were not, which might suggest that they were not yet written and come from after 70 CE. In that case they cannot have influenced the Gospels significantly. Chapters 37–71 now survive only in Ethiopic. In any case, the text involves an apocalyptic vision of eschatological judgment in which the "son of man" figure appears and is eventually identified with Enoch himself. In Enoch, the figure is essentially the same as that in Daniel 7.

Second, we turn to occurrences of the term in 2 Esdras or 4 Ezra. The original text of this no longer survives and is only known at second hand. It probably dates from the end of the first century CE. Once again, the "son of man" figure is essentially like that of Daniel 7.

Finally, in the Dead Sea Scrolls, the expression appears mostly in the plural, i.e., "sons of men," but the singular does occur (1QS XI 20–3; 1QH IV 29ff.). Generally speaking, in the scrolls the expression seems to have human and natural associations such as death, rather than other worldly associations. In addition to these three uses, there has also been much discussion of the influence of "primal man" traditions on the concept of the son of man. For example, the figure of Adam as a primal or typical representative human figure appears in Genesis, in Paul, and in Philo. Similar notions can be found in Zoroastrianism; in Christian Gnosticism; and in the Hermetic document *Poimandres* from the second century CE. There is obviously a wide range of uses and meanings here, but the apocalyptic figure of Daniel was the most influential in early Christianity.

What does all this tell us about the meaning of the expression "the Son of Man" in the Gospels? We have already noted that, with three exceptions, "the Son of Man" is only used by Jesus himself in the Gospels (or allusions to his use). The next thing to note is that in the Greek of the Gospels, the expression has a definite article: "*the* Son of Man" (*ho huios tou anthropou*). It is clear, then, that by the time the expression was used in the Gospels it had become a title of some sort. The first task here is to look at the actual uses in the Gospels. There have been many approaches to the Son of Man sayings, but it is helpful first of all to note the different emphases of the several evangelists. First, in Mark's Gospel, Son of Man is already a key feature of the theology and is used to show that Jesus is God's representative (2:10, 28); that he must suffer and die (8:31; 9:31; 10:33; 10:45); but will in due course be exalted (13:26; 14:62). The other synoptic evangelists take over many of Mark's uses but also add their own. Matthew's use of Mark and his own additions show that his emphasis is on the eschaton or end-time and the future coming of the Son of Man (see Mark 8:27 // Matt. 16:13; Mark 9:1 // Matt. 16:28; Mark 8:31 // Matt. 16:21; also Matt. 10:23; 19:28; 25:31; 26:1). Luke tends to blur the emphases already noted in Mark and Matthew and to use the expression in a more general way (see Luke 6:22; 18:8; 19:10; 21:36; 22:48). Also, by Luke's time "son of man" seems to have become more clearly a title: it has not only gained a definite article and different emphases but now seems to be a much more stable part of the tradition.

In the Fourth Gospel, Son of Man carries a very specific range of meanings and is often clearly influenced by Daniel 7:13. It occurs thirteen times, all in the first half of the Gospel (1:51; 3:13, 14; 5:27; 6:27, 53, 62; 8:28; 9:35; 12:23, 34 [twice]; 13:31). The expression is now much more clearly a christological device that indicates Jesus as one who is to suffer and die, who is a revelation of God, and who is the savior of humankind. The key occurrence of the expression is at 3:14 where it is linked up with Numbers 21:8–9. Here, the fourth evangelist links the expression "Son of Man" with language of "lifting up" and "glorification" in a reference to Jesus' death (*hupsothesetai kai doxsasthesetai*, cf. Isaiah 52:13).

In the quest for the authenticity and meaning of the Son of Man sayings, it is usually assumed that the occurrences in the synoptic Gospels are earlier than those in John and are therefore more likely to be closer to the historical Jesus and perhaps even come from him. Commentators are largely agreed that the Son of Man sayings in the synoptic Gospels fall into three main categories: first, sayings that concern the period of Jesus' ministry, e.g., at the healing of the paralytic in Mark 2: "But that you may know that the Son of Man has authority on earth to forgive sins . . ." (2:10; cf. 2:28). This is clearly a very early and basic use. The expression is present in this sense in the material common to Matthew and Luke usually known as Q, e.g., "Foxes have holes, and birds of the air have nests; but the Son of Man has nowhere to lay his head" (Matt. 8:20 // Luke 9:58; cf. Matt. 11:19 // Luke 7:34; Matt. 12:32 // Luke 12:10; and Luke 11:30); second, sayings that concern Jesus' death and resurrection (e.g., Mark 8:31; 9:31; 10:33, 45; 13:26; 14:21, 41, 62 *et par.*); and third, sayings that relate the Son of Man to the end of time (e.g., Matt. 10:23 // Luke 12:8; Matt. 25:31). There have been almost as many different views as there are scholars as to which of these sayings might actually come from Jesus himself. Some have claimed that none of the sayings come from Jesus and that he probably did not use the expression, or if he did, he did not mean anything in particular by it. On this view, all the sayings as we know them were created by the early

Christians, and the expression was given a definite article after the time of Jesus. Others have claimed that only the eschatological sayings come from Jesus but that he was referring to someone other than himself when he used the expression. Overall, there is now an almost complete *impasse* in regard to solving the problem of the authenticity of the Son of Man sayings.

A major contribution to the task of trying to solve the problems associated with the Son of Man sayings has been that of Geza Vermes. In his book *Jesus the Jew* (1973), Vermes claimed that the expression "the Son of Man" was never a title at all in the Judaism of the period in which the Gospels were written: at that time, he claims, the expression had no definite article and was simply a circumlocution for "I" or "one" (e.g., Matt. 8:20 // Luke 9:58). For Vermes, the expression would simply not have stood out in the Hebrew language anymore than "I" or "one" do in English. They were simply a self-reference. Even in Daniel 7:13 and elsewhere, Vermes claims, "son of man" was not titular and did not refer to an expected "Son of Man" figure that might be thought of as messianic. Vermes concluded, therefore, that even if Jesus did use the expression, he would not have meant anything in particular by it. The early Christians added the definite article and turned the expression into a title, although the mystery as to why they did so still remains. Vermes's insistence that it was never a title at all has done much to challenge the idea that calling Jesus "the Son of Man" was some sort of divine apocalyptic title. However, not everyone has agreed with Vermes and the matter remains unresolved.

Overall, the background and use of the expression "son of man" turn out to be complex and varied. Clearly the expression could mean simply "man" in ancient Judaism, but the use in Daniel 7:13 suggests an important representative man in the heavenly court. He is hardly divine, but he is in a significant place with a significant role in relation to God. Uses of the expression in other ancient Jewish texts are clearly influenced by Daniel 7. By the time of the Gospels, Son of Man has gained a definite article and a number of interpretations of the meaning are possible. But in many cases it is clearly influenced by Daniel 7 and means more than simply "man."

In conclusion, the expressions "son of god" and "son of man" are not so polarized in their original meanings as they came to be in later Christian theology and as they so often are in contemporary Christian usage. In fact, they did not originally carry the simple meanings "divinity" and "humanity" often associated with them today. "Son of god" in the ancient Greco-Roman and Jewish worlds could be used of anybody from ordinary people right up to the Caesar or the King of Israel. It certainly implied a special relationship with a god but it was not an exclusive title indicating divine status. A "son of god" could be any ordinary human being. In the early strands of the New Testament, the expression is specifically associated with Jesus' death and is later linked up with his pre-existence. Even though it refers to an important relation with God, however, it does not yet carry the trinitarian overtones it carries in the christology of the later councils of the church.

When we turn to the second expression, "son of man," the task of discerning a dominant meaning is even more complex, and once again there was obviously a very wide range of uses. If one use was that it meant simply "man," as in the Psalms and Ezekiel, then there is at least a different climate in Daniel 7 where the "man" appears in the heavenly court in the company of God. In the New Testament, the expression has the definite article and is now much more specifically a title associated with Jesus' suffering, death, and glorification. Furthermore, it is often clearly linked up with the figure from Daniel 7. Finally, then, the backgrounds and meanings of these two expressions are extremely broad and complex, and in relation to Jesus it is irresponsible simply to equate "Son of God" with his divinity and "Son of Man" with his humanity.

FIVE

MESSIANIC MYSTERY

MARK'S APOPHATIC CHRISTOLOGY

It is well known that in the synoptic Gospels, and especially in Mark, Jesus frequently tells people not to say who he is or what has happened to them when he has healed them. It is also well known that on other occasions he tells them to go out and tell people what has happened to them, or that they do so anyway. A single reading of the Gospels shows that there is something odd about this. How could Jesus' miracles be kept secret and at the same time be widely known? The problem is especially acute in Mark's Gospel and has become known as the "messianic secret." It arises specifically out of the combination of secrecy about who Jesus is with moments of revelation of his identity.

For centuries commentators assumed that this secrecy and revelation theme in Mark's Gospel arose because historically Jesus had only revealed his identity to the disciples gradually. In the nineteenth century, however, the German New Testament scholar Wilhelm Wrede (1859–1906) saw that there was more to it than this. He claimed that although the secrecy motif had arisen in specific historical circumstances, its purpose was primarily apologetic and theological. Nevertheless, in spite of Wrede's theories dominating discussions of the secrecy theme in Mark, its theological side has sometimes still been neglected.

This chapter is not concerned with why the secrecy motif arose in the first place, or with how Mark edited his material in relation to it. Nor do I wish to attempt an overall "solution" to the secrecy problem. Rather, my concern here is to draw attention to the peculiar climate the secrecy theme creates in Mark's narrative and to claim that it is best seen in terms of "revelation," "mystery," and "apophasis." In order to do this, I shall first outline and challenge the view that Jesus' identity in Mark's Gospel is revealed only gradually. Second, I take some cues from the work of Wrede and note subsequent developments; and third, I examine the words "revelation," "mystery," and "apophasis."

The "Gradual Revelation" Theory

The traditional view of the portrayal of Jesus in Mark's Gospel was that there is a gradual revelation of who he is as the narrative progresses. This view maintained that in the first half of the Gospel, Jesus' real identity is mostly hidden, while in the second half it is mostly revealed. The turning point or watershed on this view is the incident at Caesarea Philippi (8:27–33) in which Jesus' messianic status is made clear. By the time of the cross and the resurrection in the final chapters of the Gospel, Jesus' full identity is out. The view that Jesus' identity is only gradually revealed in Mark's Gospel was usually supported by the claim that this is how it had been historically with Jesus himself: he had chosen not to let on who he was, either in order to avoid Jewish overreaction or because he thought people ought not to be confronted with his real identity all at once.

The view that Jesus' identity is only gradually revealed in Mark's Gospel was based on key texts from the Gospel that identified two crucial themes: that of hiddenness or secrecy in the first half of the Gospel, and that of openness or revelation in the second. In the first half of the Gospel, in which Jesus' identity is largely hidden, Jesus silences the demons who recognize him (1:25, 34; 3:11ff.) and people he has healed (1:43ff.; 5:43; 7:36; 8:26). There is also obscurity and hidden teaching in his parables (esp. 4:10–12), and the disciples frequently misunderstand who he is (1:22; 4:41; 6:52; 7:17ff.; 8:21). Toward the middle of the Gospel, a blind man at Bethsaida cannot see clearly even after he has been healed, but then does so after a second healing (8:22–26; cf. 10:46–52). This incident is often seen as the moment when secrecy in relation to Jesus' identity turns more obviously to revelation. This incident is then followed by that at Caesarea Philippi in which Jesus asks his disciples, "Who do people say I am?" Peter's reply, "You are the Christ" (8:27–33), is reckoned to be the moment when Jesus' identity is out. The question that has been asked at 4:41, "Who then is this?" is finally answered. After this incident it is clear to everyone that Jesus is the Messiah.

In the second half of the Gospel, Jesus' identity is much more in the open. The Transfiguration makes his nature and mission clear (9:2–10), and the so-called passion predictions illustrate what sort of Messiah he is (8:31; 9:31; 10:33, 45). Jesus is now "the Lord" (11:3) and is almost certainly the "beloved son" of the parable of the vineyard (12:1–12). In the Passion Narrative Jesus replies positively to the high priest's question "Are you the Christ?" (14:61–62), and at the crucifixion, the Gentile centurion proclaims "Truly this man was a/the Son of God" (15:39), bringing the revelation of Jesus' identity to a climax. Finally, the empty tomb story confirms everything that has happened in the Gospel: Jesus is the crucified and risen messiah and Son of God, and the secret is fully out!

However convincing this view of Mark's Gospel might seem, it is oversimplistic and misleading. Key texts are ignored and the overall thrust of the narrative is missed. Mark's Gospel simply doesn't divide neatly into two halves in this way. However, this view does at least identify two basic themes in the narrative: that of hiddenness or secrecy and that of openness or revelation. Rather than operating separately in the two halves of the Gospel, however, these two themes are intertwined in a single christological dynamic in which Jesus' real identity is both revealed and hidden. One of the first people to see the full complexity of Mark's Gospel in this respect was Wilhelm Wrede, who in the nineteenth century emphasized the "messianic secret" in Mark's Gospel as a specific theological motif.

Working with Wrede

Wilhelm Wrede wrote his work *Das Messiasgeheimnis in den Evangelien* in 1901 (ET 1971, *The Messianic Secret in the Gospels*). His book has been widely interpreted and misinterpreted over the years and has provoked numerous conflicting reactions. Although much of the detail of his work has been rejected, his overall perspective has been adopted by most commentators. Wrede began by observing that it was unlikely that some of the events as recounted in Mark's Gospel could really be historical. How could the healing of Jairus's daughter in Mark 5, for example, be kept a secret when such news would have spread rapidly in the local community? Wrede concluded that the secrecy theme in Mark should be seen as a theological and apologetic motif rather than as something historical. He maintained that the secrecy motif had arisen because whereas the earliest Christians believed that Jesus only became Messiah at his resurrection, later Christians believed he had been Messiah all along. This situation left a messianic silence in Jesus' life that had to be explained. The secrecy motif was then injected into the tradition and eventually found its way into Mark's Gospel. In addition to the major texts that have already been noted in the previous section, Wrede saw that there are occasions in the first half of the Gospel when Jesus' identity is well known (1:45; 5:20), and occasions in the second half when there is still secrecy and misunderstanding (9:9; 9:30f.; 10:32). Nor is the Caesarea Philippi incident such a clear picture of revelation as is often assumed: there is still confusion on that occasion about the nature of Jesus' messiahship. Peter does not understand the true sense of "Christ" and is condemned by Jesus as satanic in Mark. As a result of his observations, Wrede concluded that two themes of secrecy and revelation flow together throughout the narrative.

One text that Wrede saw as central was Mark 9:9, which indicates that the secret will be revealed at the resurrection. It certainly seems that 9:9 is central to understanding the secrecy motif, but not in the way Wrede and others thought. It is worth looking closely at what actually happens in Mark's empty tomb story in order to see how it is theologically central for the secrecy theme. It is frequently observed that both the beginning and the ending of Mark's Gospel are odd. The beginning is sudden and abrupt, and Jesus appears with no biographical introduction. The conclusion at 16:8 also seems abrupt and enigmatic. Most commentators are agreed that this is the original ending to the Gospel, but in Greek it ends in mid-sentence and feels unfinished. However, what has not been acknowledged in many of the discussions of the resurrection and the secrecy theme in Mark is that the empty tomb story in 16:1–8 brings the whole Gospel to an end on a note of silence and fear. It is certainly a key moment in the narrative and theology of the Gospel, but that key note is one of fear and silence and there are no resurrection appearances. This indicates that the theme of secrecy is itself part of the message of the resurrection. Indeed, it seems that the empty tomb story is the final exposure of the combined secrecy and revelation theme: what is revealed in the resurrection is still something substantially enigmatic, silent, and hidden.

In the years since Wrede wrote his book and in the wake of more recent redaction and narrative criticism of the Gospels, it has become increasingly clear that Mark's narrative is a multilayered tapestry of intertwined secrecy and revelation motifs that can be approached from a number of different perspectives. For example, one might view the question from the angle of the author, or that of the different characters within the text. From the point of view of the author, there is in one sense no "secrecy" about who

Jesus is. Mark knows what he intends to say about Jesus before he begins to write his Gospel (cf. 1:1). He knows what is going to happen at the end, at the empty tomb. The demons also know who Jesus is. Disciples, Jesus' family, scribes and Pharisees, however, all misunderstand. From the overall perspective of the reader, however, the rich layers of secrecy and revelation can be seen to create a climate that holds the whole fabric of the Gospel together. As the narrative proceeds, the intertwined secrecy-revelation theme runs fugally through the Gospel, producing a single theme of "secrecy-revelation."

Whereas the old two-part "gradual revelation" view ultimately undermines Mark's christology, it can now be seen that there is a single two-part theme permeating the whole Gospel. This single two-part motif creates a christological climate in Mark in which the element of hiddenness dominates. This suggests that the theme should be seen in terms of "mystery," "revelation," and "apophatic theology" rather than of secrecy.

Although Wrede's overall concerns were rather different from those here, it is nevertheless interesting to note that in translating Wrede's German book title, *The Messianic Mystery in the Gospels* would be preferable to *The Messianic Secret in the Gospels*; his word *Geheimnis* is far better rendered into English as "mystery" than as "secret." With this in mind, it is worth looking closely at the notion of "mystery" and related words in order to see what light these might shed on Mark's christology.

Mystery, Revelation, and Apophatic Theology

The idea that the "messianic secret" in Mark's Gospel should be understood in terms of mystery, revelation, and apophatic theology obviously begs the question, "What do these words mean?" The Greek word for mystery is *musterion*. It certainly carries the sense of something hidden; something not yet known or revealed. The verb *mueo* probably means "to close" and refers to something fundamentally hidden or stopped. However, there is more to *mus-*

terion than just "secrecy." In the New Testament, "mystery" is used twenty-one times in the writings of Paul but hardly ever in the Gospels. In Paul it indicates the hidden things of God which will be revealed at the end of time. In 1 Corinthians 15:51 Paul writes, "Lo! I tell you a mystery (*musterion*)" when speaking of the eschatological significance of the resurrection. In the Gospel tradition, "mystery" in the singular occurs only once: in relation to the parables and the kingdom of God (Mark 4:11 *et par.*). In spite of this, however, it is a central concept that broods over the Gospel teaching on the parables and the kingdom. In Mark, the mystery of the kingdom of God involves not only something mysterious and hidden, but also something revealed and known. Indeed, the word "mystery" does seem to be an appropriate word to use of Mark's overall christology, especially as it influences not only his concept of the kingdom of God but also his basic concept of Jesus the preacher of the kingdom.

One helpful way to understand "mystery" is to contrast it with "secret," "problem," and "paradox." In principle, secrets and problems can be made known or be solved. A state secret, for example, might become known to the public or to other nations; a mathematical problem might be solved through the use of a formula. A paradox, whether it is defined as "an apparent contradiction" or as "a real contradiction," can usually be explained. The "most ingenious paradox" of Gilbert and Sullivan's *Pirates of Penzance*, for example, is that Frederic was born in a leap year and the paradox is perfectly explainable. Mysteries, however, are different from secrets, problems, and paradoxes. A mystery is relational and experiential; it is "entered into" or "inhabited" rather than uncovered, solved, or explained. The mysteries of love, evil, marriage, or of a sacrament, for example, will need to be "entered into" in order to be known. With these distinctions in mind it is clear that the so-called "messianic secret" in Mark would be better understood as a "messianic mystery" in that it is a reality to be entered into rather than a secret to be uncovered. Wrede used the word "Messiah" to refer to Jesus' overall identity and not only to the stricter sense in which he was Messiah. It seems reasonable enough to continue this usage and to speak of "messianic mystery" in relation to Mark's christology.

We have seen in the first section of this chapter that the word "revelation" has been used of Mark's christology. The sense in which the word is actually appropriate to Mark's Gospel is, however, rather different from its use in the "gradual revelation" theory. It is not that Jesus' identity is "gradually revealed" or uncovered, but that he is a revelation of God throughout and that this is part of the "messianic mystery" motif. Like "mystery," the word "revelation" can carry different meanings. The primary meaning of "revelation" is that something hidden has been made known. In this sense "revelation" is close etymologically to "apocalypse," the Greek word meaning to "draw back" or "uncover" what is hidden. The theology of Mark's Gospel has its roots in apocalyptic, especially the Book of Daniel where the Son of Man is part of the revelation of the heavenly court and the purposes of God. It is not surprising, therefore, that "revelation" is an appropriate word to use of Mark's christology. In the Christian tradition generally, the word has often referred to God's revelation in nature, experience, reason, the Bible, or in language.

There has also been talk of "general" and "special" revelation. At the root of much of this there has been a strong sense that God is still substantially hidden even when he is revealed. The most obvious case of this is the revelation of God to Moses in the burning bush in Exodus 3. Although God is revealed, he is still essentially hidden, and the event constitutes the revelation of a mystery. This is not a case of a secret exposed, a problem solved, or a paradox explained. What is revealed to Moses is still hidden. In the same way, in Mark's Gospel Jesus' identity is revealed but still hidden. The interplay of secrecy, revelation, seeing, not seeing, hiddenness, and misunderstanding contributes to a strong sense that Mark is presenting Jesus as a revelation of God. When Jesus' identity is revealed, there is silence and fear in response. This is clearly the case after the resurrection in 16:1–8. Because Mark deals in enigma and hiddenness more than in openness and clarity where the identity of Jesus is concerned, his christology can usefully be seen in terms of "revelation."

Finally, what of the overall claim that Mark's christology is "apophatic"? Apophatic theology is theology that proceeds by negation. That is to say, it admits that even though it knows God through revelation, human language is limited in its attempt to describe him. It acknowledges the hiddenness, mystery, and unknowability of God and the importance of silence in theology and spirituality. The apophatic way is sometimes known as the *via negativa* or "negative way." By contrast, "cataphatic theology" emphasizes what can be said or known about God. It emphasizes God's revealed nature and knowability. The cataphatic way is sometimes called the *via positiva* or "positive way." In the Christian tradition the apophatic and cataphatic ways have often gone together in a healthy combination. Frequently, however, as in mystical theology, the apophatic way has dominated and the emphasis has been on hiddenness and mystery. The idea that human knowledge of God is limited in this life but is clear in the next can be found already in St. Paul (1 Cor. 13:12), and it developed considerably in the writings of Origen, Pseudo-Dionysius, and Thomas Aquinas. Indeed it can also be found in the mystical traditions of Judaism and Islam. However, there has been a divergence of views regarding what will be revealed about God at the end of time. Some theologians have followed Paul in believing that God will be known "face to face" in the end. Others, for example Karl Rahner, have emphasized God's ultimate unknowability and have claimed that even in the final eschatological revelation, God will be encountered as mystery. Such an encounter would naturally result in human silence, denial, wonder, and amazement. This type of experience lies at the heart of the Christian mystical tradition and of apophatic theology.

It should now be clear that words such as mystery, revelation, and apophatic are wholly appropriate when used of the theology of Mark's Gospel. Throughout the Gospel, Jesus' identity is both revealed and yet hidden. The entire Gospel confronts the reader with enigma and hiddenness. Even at the empty tomb, the ultimate eschatological revelation, there is emptiness, silence, and fear. All this speaks of a theology in which there is certainly revelation, but a revelation that is dominated by the experience of the hiddenness of God. The notion that the nature of Jesus is ultimately mysterious even when it is revealed, and hidden even when it has been made known, gives sense to the expression "apophatic christology" here. The two-part theme of hiddenness and revelation together in Mark, with the emphasis on the hiddenness, clearly indicates that Mark's is an "apophatic christology."

Why would he be concerned with such a christology? It has often been claimed that Mark emphasized the cross in order to correct false beliefs about Jesus' messiahship and possibly to counter the idea that Jesus was predominantly a divine man (*theios aner*). It is equally possible, then, that Mark used an apophatic christology to counter beliefs he considered inadequate.

In Mark's Gospel there are occasions when Jesus tells people to be quiet about who he is and what he has done, and there are also occasions when he tells them to go out and tell everyone, or they do so anyway. These themes of hiddenness and openness permeate the entire narrative, creating a mysterious climate around Jesus. Other themes such as the misunderstanding of the disciples and the obscure teaching on parables add to this general climate. However, the old idea that Jesus' identity is gradually revealed over the whole Gospel is inadequate. Rather, there is a specific christology operative throughout. Wrede drew attention to the rich complexity of the secret in Mark and claimed that it was primarily a theological and apologetic motif, but there has still been too little discussion of its real christological significance. The single two-part theme of hiddenness-openness or secrecy-revelation alerts the reader to a constant oscillation in Mark's presentation of Jesus which indicates a climate of mystery, revelation, and apophasis rather than secret, problem, or paradox. Even at the empty tomb, the ultimate eschatological revelation, there is emptiness, silence, and fear. All this speaks of a theology in which there is certainly revelation, but a revelation that is dominated by the experience of the hiddenness of God. The notion that the nature of Jesus is ultimately mysterious even when it is revealed, and hidden even when it has been made known, gives sense to the expression "apophatic christology" here. I conclude, therefore, that the so-called "messianic secret" in Mark's Gospel should be called the "messianic mystery," and also that since Mark's presentation of Jesus emphasizes mystery and enigma more than openness, it is quite legitimate to call his christology "apophatic."

SIX

JESUS THE BREAD OF GOD

THE EUCHARIST AS METAPHOR IN JOHN 6

The suggestion that some of the language in chapter 6 of St. John's Gospel (in particular verses 51–58) should be interpreted metaphorically usually sets off alarm bells in the minds and hearts of Christian believers. The idea that the words of Jesus, "unless you eat the flesh of the Son of Man and drink his blood, you have no life in you" (6:53), are metaphorical, is tantamount, they say, to denying the real presence of Christ in the Eucharist. This widespread misunderstanding arises largely because of a popular assumption that metaphors are basically false, and also because of a lack of familiarity with the place of John 6 in the Fourth Gospel as a whole. It also arises because fundamental connections between Jesus, the eucharist, and baptism are overlooked. The aim of this chapter is to show that the bread, flesh, and blood language in John 6 should be interpreted metaphorically, and that this is a "theological gain" rather than a loss. I will also indicate that christology, eucharist, and baptism are all fundamentally related in the Fourth Gospel. I shall briefly consider, therefore: first, the background and content of John 6; second, the nature of metaphor; and third, the eucharist as metaphor in John 6.

John 6: Background and Content

To what extent is John 6 really about the eucharist? The first task is to see this chapter in its wider context in the Fourth Gospel. It is sometimes suggested that the fourth evangelist plays down his interest in the Last Supper (ch. 13) and in the baptism of Jesus (ch. 1) by omitting important material which we know from elsewhere. For example, he has no Last Supper scene as such, in the style of Matthew, Mark, and Luke; no bread and wine; and no words of institution. There is also no direct narrative account of the baptism of Jesus by John earlier in the Gospel. However, these observations alert the reader to a rather more important dynamic in the narrative than at first meets the eye. It looks as though this Gospel writer has deliberately left the eucharistic details out of the narrative in chapter 13, and then put his teaching on the eucharist in the Bread of Life discourse in chapter 6, and possibly also in the Vine discourse in chapter 15. The supper scene in chapter 13 is now dominated by the washing of the disciples' feet. Through this, the disciples are initiated into a life of humility and service, and the water with which they are washed evokes their baptism into Jesus' suffering and death. All this reminds members of the Johannine community of the close connection between Jesus himself, baptism, and the eucharist. By "eucharist" in this discussion, I mean simply the early Christian meal that used bread and wine.

The content of John 6 and its wider context in the New Testament must also be noted. John 6 itself consists of a number of distinct sections: (a) an introduction, indicating a Passover setting (vv. 1–4); (b) the Feeding of the Five Thousand (vv. 5–15); (c) the Walking on Water (vv. 16–24); (d) material relating to manna and the Son of Man (vv. 25–34); (e) the Bread of Life discourse (vv. 35–65); and (f) a conclusion (vv. 66–71). This material includes bread, water, flesh, and blood imagery, but our primary interest is in the bread. In order to focus the wider picture into which the bread imagery in John 6 fits, it is first worth noting other places in the New Testament where bread appears. The important narratives are: the Last Supper (Matt. 26:26–29; Mark 14:22–25; Luke 22:14–23; 1 Cor. 11:23–32); the Feeding of the Five Thousand (Matt. 14:15–21; Mark 6:35–44; Luke 9:10–17); and the meal at Emmaus (Luke 24:30–32). Further material relating to grain and bread, wine and vines, and meals is also of interest here (e.g., Mark 2:23–28 *et par.*; 4:2–9 *et par.*; 4:26–29; 12:1–12 *et par.*; 14:3–9 *et par.*; John 2:1–11; 12:24; 15:1–8), as is the practice of "breaking bread" in Acts (2:42, 46). Although there are different views of the degree to which these texts are intended to be understood as eucharistic, they all form an important part of the wider discussion of John 6.

Two interesting issues arise immediately from John 6:5–15. One concerns the so-called "fourfold action" with the bread (taking, blessing, breaking, and giving); the other is the Greek word *eucharistesas* (when he had given thanks). First, while the synoptic Last Supper narratives have a "fourfold action" with the bread, John 6:5–15 has a "threefold action" (taking, thanking, and giving; cf. 1 Cor. 11:23–24). However, in the longer version of Luke's Last Supper scene, Jesus takes a cup first, then bread, then another cup, and the *Didache* (an early Christian text of the first or second century) refers first to a cup and then to bread. There was clearly a diversity of eucharistic practice in the early centuries, and we cannot conclude, as some have, that the threefold action in John 6 is somehow not eucharistic. Second, some people have claimed that the Greek word *eucharistesas* in John 6:11 specifically indicates the eucharist. However, this word was not a technical term at the time; it simply meant "give thanks" and was synonymous with "bless" (cf. Mark 14:22, 23). Its use in John 6, therefore, cannot determine that the fourth evangelist has specifically eucharistic intentions in mind there (cf. John 11:41). In the end, whatever we conclude about these two features, a strong sense persists that these verses do carry a eucharistic message.

The most controversial words in John 6 are those concerning "eating the flesh" of the Son of Man in verses 51–58. These verses are the most difficult in the chapter and there is certainly something striking about them. Although some commentators have understandably suggested that they were added later, it is possible to see them as an integral part of the chapter. The difficult words here are "flesh" (*sarx*) and "eat" (*trogo*). The idea of "eating flesh and drinking blood" certainly seems to give the verses, and maybe the chapter, a specifically eucharistic feel, and it is here that many people wish to find a direct reference to the eucharist. However, in the Greek text, the word for flesh in these verses is *sarx* and not *soma* or "body" as it is in the synoptic Last Supper Narratives and in 1 Corinthians 11. If John 6 were consciously intended to be about the eucharist, then the writer might have deliberately used the word *soma* in order to make the connection with these other narratives or traditions, but he has not done so. It can be argued, of course, that whereas *soma* means "body," *sarx* refers to the whole human person and is therefore a better word here. Also, it is *sarx* or flesh which the Word or Logos has taken in 1:14. Even so, it is strange, if verses 51–58 are supposed to be about the eucharist, that we are told in verse 63 that "the flesh is of no avail." Perhaps the eucharistic imagery in all this is intended to be understood less specifically than is often thought.

The other significant word in verses 51–58 is "eat." In John 6 generally, the word used for eating is *phagomai*, which means simply "eat." In verses 51–58, the writer also uses *trogo* (instead of *phagomai* or *esthio* which he might have used) in relation to eating the flesh of the Son of Man. The word *trogo* means more than simply eating; it has the sense of "munching" or "crunching" the food. The question here is whether there is any real significance in this word, or whether the change is merely stylistic. Some have seen it as a deliberately "anti-docetic" word aimed at those who would spiritualize the eating at the eucharist. The other occurrence of this word in the Fourth Gospel is in the supper scene at 13:18. Soon afterwards, in 13:30, Judas eats the bread and goes straight out into the darkness. There have been different views of this verse, and some have seen it as a particularly powerful case of Johannine irony: Do not the members of the Johannine community (and we?) do the same? In John 6, however, it is not immediately obvious that *trogo* must refer directly to the elements of the eucharist. In fact, if it is understood in a metaphorical sense it seems to be much more in keeping with the thrust of the passage. In view of these observations concerning particular actions and words, it seems fair to say that the eucharistic imagery in John 6 is used in a much looser and more suggestive manner than is often thought. The author does not wish simply to refer to the eucharist here; he has a much more subtle theological purpose in mind.

If the eucharist as such is not the fourth evangelist's main concern here, then what is? The answer, of course, is Jesus himself, the Son of Man, the "bread of God" which has come down from heaven to give life to the world. The concept of the Son of Man has a complex background in Daniel 7:13 and elsewhere, but overall it associates Jesus with suffering and humility. It is a key Johannine expression and is used in this chapter in connection with ascending and descending (vv. 38, 62). The theme of the "manna in the wilderness" is also fundamental here: the background to this lies in Exodus 16, Psalm 78, and elsewhere. The manna is God's food for his people, it is the bread of God. For the fourth evangelist, however, it is now Jesus, not Moses, who not only gives the bread but is himself the bread of God: "the bread of God is that which comes down from heaven (v. 33). This is the bread which gives life to those who believe. The food which is to be eaten is the food of Jesus' suffering and death. The implication of all this is that Jesus the bread of God is the main subject of concern in John 6; eucharistic imagery is then used as a metaphor through which Jesus' real identity might be glimpsed. Johannine Christians doubtless already knew of the importance of the eucharist, but they had forgotten its connection with baptism and Jesus the suffering Son of Man. The fourth evangelist arranged the material in his Gospel in order to give his supper scene in chapter 13 a baptismal focus, and his eucharistic teaching in chapter 6 a christological focus. In doing this he reminded his community that christology, baptism, and eucharist are three aspects of a single reality.

The Nature of Metaphor

The suggestion that the bread imagery in John 6 and especially the words of Jesus in verses 51–58 concerning eating and drinking his flesh and blood, should be interpreted metaphorically, raises the obvious question, "What then is a metaphor?" People react negatively to the suggestion that this language is metaphorical because of a basic misunderstanding of metaphor itself. Everyone is familiar with metaphors and they influence language and perception at many different levels. However, in everyday conversation, metaphors are often thought of as false, and are contrasted with "literal" or "true" language. So it is with the claim here in relation to John 6. If Jesus' words, "he who eats my flesh and drinks my blood has eternal life" (v. 54), are metaphorical, surely this implies that the words are not really true. But metaphors are richer and subtler than that, and to imagine that the claim that language is metaphorical is a denial of its truth, is a gross misunderstanding. Metaphors can sometimes articulate truth far more adequately than literal language, and in any case both metaphorical language and literal language can be either true or false.

Metaphors are part of a wide network of figurative language that includes images, symbols, allegories, analogies, and similes. The word "metaphor" itself comes from two Greek words: *meta* (across) and *pherein* (to carry). Together they mean "to carry across" in the sense of a transference. There are two elements at work in a metaphor; one thing is transferred or carried over into the other. Unlike so-called literal language in which words carry their most obvious or straightforward meaning, metaphor has two elements which come together: the thing referred to, and the image used in referring to it. In his *Poetics*, Aristotle says that metaphor is "giving the thing a name that belongs to something else" (1457b). In metaphor, one thing is spoken of in terms of another. The metaphor, unlike the simile, contains elements of identity, truth, and falsity. When we say, for example, that "John is a pig" or "Her face was a picture," there is a specific thrust of meaning that is lacking in the simile "John is like a pig," or "Her face was like a picture." In the metaphor, John is not *like* a pig, he *is* one! In the same way, the statement "Jesus is the bread of life" combines two elements, producing a specific tension that trades on a combination of truth and falsity. John is not literally a pig, and Jesus is not literally bread, but something is captured in these metaphors that is specific and cannot be said in literal language. Of course, the simple form of metaphor, calling one thing another thing ("A is a B") is not its only form. When Jack "upsets the apple cart" or Susan "puts the cat among the pigeons," the simple statement of identity has given way to speaking of one thing in terms of something else in a subtler and more developed manner. An even more complex process is at work when metaphors persist in lengthy narratives, such as poems, plays, and novels.

There are many different views of what metaphors are, but philosophers, theologians, and others agree more and more that they are not mere decorations: they are vehicles of insight and revelation that say things no other language, least of all literal language, can ever say; their revelatory power enables them to make new connections and to see new dimensions; in religion, theology, and faith, they are indispensable; and in trying to speak of God, Christ, or the eucharist, they are the most adequate tools. The revelatory power of metaphor is certainly at work in the Fourth Gospel: when Jesus says that he is the "door of the sheep," the "true vine," or the "bread of life," the metaphors reveal truths and insights that cannot be spoken of in other language. To claim that Jesus' words in John 6 are metaphorical, then, is to claim much, much more even than to claim that they are literally true: it is to claim that they have an important revelatory power.

The Eucharist as Metaphor in John 6

With this revelatory power of metaphor in mind, let us return to John 6 to see what is happening there in relation to Jesus and the eucharist. We have seen that in metaphor one thing is spoken of using the name of another thing. In John 6, Jesus speaks of himself using the language of bread, flesh, and blood. He *himself* is the bread of life. The other "I am" sayings in the Fourth Gospel bear out the same sense: for example, Jesus says "I am the door of the sheep" (10:7); "I am the good shepherd" (10:11); and "I am the vine" (15:5), but these are not literal references to doors, shepherds, and vines. They are metaphors that refer to Jesus himself. The vine language in chapter 15 is rarely thought to be a direct reference to the eucharist itself, even if it is thought to use a eucharistic image. The same is true of the bread and eucharist imagery in chapter 6: it is about Jesus himself. The water imagery in the Fourth Gospel is also interesting in this respect: there is no "I am" saying directly relating to water, but Jesus is himself clearly the water of life (4:13f.; 6:35; 7:37). However, this is not to be taken literally; it is a metaphor for Jesus himself. The same is true also of the bread imagery. It is noteworthy that the bread of life metaphor is particularly powerful among the "I am" sayings of the Fourth Gospel precisely because it draws upon something that was already extremely powerful in Christian life—the eucharist. The same might also be true of the vine imagery. For this reason these "I am" sayings have a far greater impact than the others.

For the difficult verses 51–58, including "unless you eat the flesh of the Son of Man and drink his blood, you have no life in you" (v. 53), the key question is, Do these words actually refer to bread and wine, the elements of the eucharist, or do they refer to Jesus himself? This is the point at which many people find the claim that the language is metaphorical most difficult. Even if the rest of the chapter is to be understood metaphorically, they say, surely these verses are literal references to the bread and wine of the eucharist. Surely the use of the Greek word *trogo* underlines the fact that these words do actually refer to partaking of the eucharistic elements. In fact, however, this does not seem to be the case. Jesus himself is the subject of the chapter, and the real reference here in verses 51–58 is still Jesus. Indeed, in this very section, after speaking of eating and drinking his flesh and blood, Jesus refers to the "bread which came down from heaven" (v. 58), and he himself is the one who descends and ascends (vv. 38, 41,

62). The language of eating and drinking the flesh and blood, therefore, is eucharistic language used metaphorically to refer to Jesus; "munching" and "crunching" is not a literal reference to eating the bread of the eucharist, but a metaphorical reference to Jesus. The sense of the language is eucharistic, while its reference is Jesus himself. This interpretation of some of the language of John 6 is also in line with a sense of the unity of the chapter: the subject throughout is Jesus the bread of God.

In conclusion, the alarm bells that usually ring out at the suggestion that some of the language of John 6 is metaphorical can remain silent. Metaphors speak of one thing in terms of another, and have a special revelatory capacity. The close association of Jesus with the eucharist in Christian experience certainly gives the eucharistic metaphor in John 6 an unusual power, but this is also the reason why it is so often taken literally. As we have seen, the real subject of the material throughout John 6 is Jesus himself. He is the subject of the Bread of Life discourse, including verses 51–58, and he himself is the "bread of God." He is spoken of in terms of bread and of the eucharist, but he himself is the focus. Christian familiarity with the eucharist has often obscured its place as metaphor in the narrative of John 6, but a metaphorical interpretation is not a denial of the real presence of Christ in the eucharist. Indeed, John 6 is not primarily "about" the eucharist in that sense, it is about Jesus the bread of God, and it uses eucharistic language of him. For the fourth evangelist, to eat and drink Jesus' flesh and blood is not first of all to receive the eucharistic elements as such, but to receive the Logos made flesh; to be baptized into the life of the suffering Son of Man; and to "munch" and "crunch" metaphorically on that incarnate life. In arranging his material in the Gospel in a specific way, and in choosing his words carefully, the writer reminds his community, and his modern readers, of the cost of discipleship, and of how christology, eucharist, and baptism are all related to each other. There is certainly need for alarm bells in all this, but of a rather different kind from the ones usually heard.

SEVEN

THE PARABLE OF THE PRUDENT STEWARD

A QUESTION OF IDENTITY IN LUKE 16:1–13

The story of the rich man and his steward in Luke 16:1–13 is usually known as the Parable of the Unjust Steward. This parable is not often discussed among students of the New Testament, probably because it is the most difficult of the synoptic parables to understand and interpret. Preachers tend to shy away from it because it seems to commend bad behavior with money, while commentators are not even sure where the story ends, let alone what it means! Furthermore, it is notoriously difficult to establish what the main character, the steward, is really doing and why he is commended for his actions. On the face of it, a steward who has been dismissed acts quickly in order to secure a future for himself after he has lost his job. He appears to fiddle the books and reduce people's debts in order to make friends who will look after him later. The odd thing is that he is then commended for his actions.

If we look closely at the historical background to the story, a number of questions come into view. Are the steward's actions really unjust? Is he portrayed in the story as an example to follow, or as one to avoid? Is there irony in his commendation? In fact, this parable has been interpreted in so many different ways that it has received a number of different titles in addition to the well-known one. Depending upon commentators' final interpretations of the story, the "Unjust Steward" has been renamed the "Dishonest Manager," the "Clever Rascal," the "Crafty Steward," the "Steward of Unrighteousness," or perhaps most appropriately, as we shall see, the "Prudent Steward." In this chapter, I first consider the traditional approach to this parable that has come to dominate its interpretation. This raises some basic exegetical issues that will provoke a closer examination of the background to the story. I then look at some historical and literary issues that will help shed some light on what the steward is actually doing and what the overall concern of the parable might be.

The Traditional Interpretation

The traditional name of the parable in Luke 16:1–13 in the modern period has been the Parable of the Unjust Steward. This well-known name has arisen out of the interpretation of the parable that has dominated the scholarly and devotional reading of this text since the nineteenth century. Before outlining this interpretation, it is worth observing what the narrative includes. There are two sections to consider: (1) the main part of the story in verses 1–8a; and (2) a collection of sayings in verses 8b-13. How these verses relate to each other and exactly where the join really comes is unclear and will be discussed later. First, who are the main characters? There are three: the rich man, the steward, and the debtors. There are also: those who bring the charges against the steward in the first place; those who hear the parable, especially those within Luke's narrative; and the disciples of Jesus (v. 1), the tax collectors, sinners, and Pharisees (v. 14), who already form the wider audience when the parable opens (15:1). All of these people play a part in how the story might be understood.

With these characters in mind we can now outline the sequence of events. The rich man (also referred to in the parable as the *kurios* or "lord") has a steward (*oikonomon*), and charges are brought to him that the steward is wasting his master's goods. The steward is called and told to turn in his accounts and is then dismissed. In a soliloquy section, typical of Luke, the steward then considers his options: he is not strong enough to dig and is too proud to beg. Instead he summons the debtors and reduces their debts. One debtor owing a hundred measures of oil gets the amount reduced to fifty; the second owing a hundred measures of wheat gets the amount reduced to eighty. At this point the "lord" commends the "unjust steward" (*ton oikonomon tes adikias*) because of his prudence (*phronimos*). Although it is not 100 percent clear, this seems to be the natural end of the story. Verses 8b–13 then consist of a series of sayings that relate in one way or another to the main events of the parable. The key themes of these sayings are: wisdom, faithfulness, and money in relation to God, culminating in the sharp polarization between God and mammon in verse 13. Almost any of the themes in the two sections of the narrative could be claimed to be the central theme of the parable, and the passage presents a kaleidoscope of possibilities for interpretation.

The interpretation that has come to dominate Christian reading of this parable is that the steward is basically dishonest and unjust and has fiddled his master's books by reducing the amount owed by the debtors in order to make friends who will look after him when he finally leaves his job. Indeed, this behavior is what the commendation by the master in verse 9 seems to be encouraging. On this reading, the steward is already unjust when the parable opens, and this is why he is being dismissed. His actions in the center of the parable only make matters worse. The commendation in verse 9 is, however, problematical. On this view, it is usually assumed that the "Lord" who commends the steward is Jesus, who is called "the Lord" frequently in Luke's Gospel. If there is a problem that Jesus is commending dishonest and unjust behavior, then the answer is that the steward is actually being commended for his prudence, shrewdness, and wisdom in a difficult situation (*phronimos*). The message of the parable is then perceived to be aimed at the disciples, who must behave in the same way at the time of eschatological judgment. On this view, it is not the steward's dishonesty that is being held up by Jesus, but his wisdom and foresight in a crisis. Subsequent readers of the story should then take up this message and apply it to their spiritual lives. On this view alone, then, we could claim that the steward's prudence is the key issue and dismiss his dishonesty as irrelevant. However, if we were to read the parable more specifically in its historical context and look more closely at the actual wording, it would show that the steward may not actually be unjust or dishonest in his central actions at all. Moreover, it may not be Jesus who commends him. In fact, although the steward may have been dishonest in his initial actions and is therefore unjust, he could have been acting in a perfectly just manner in his later actions and could have been commended by the rich man, who is also called "lord" in the sense of "master" or "boss." As the initial actions are not the center of the parable (we don't even know what they are), it is the later actions that should give the steward his title. He should, therefore, be called the "prudent steward" rather than the "unjust steward." Let us look more closely at the historical and literary issues.

Historical and Literary Issues

Although the traditional interpretation of this parable has dominated discussions, a fuller understanding of the historical, economic, and legal backgrounds of the parable suggests other possibilities concerning what the steward is doing. The work of J. D. M. Derrett has been instrumental in raising awareness of the background here, although we still lack enough detailed knowledge to solve all the problems. The first thing is to read the parable in the light of the social and legal positions of the characters involved. It is usually thought that the steward himself was probably a freeman rather than a slave and was, in any case, a figure thoroughly at one with his master. In such relationships, the master usually abided by the actions of the steward and the steward was completely in charge of his master's affairs. The steward would have represented his master completely in dealing with all his affairs, and the master would have had complete trust in the steward until things went wrong. In this story, of course, things have already gone wrong when the parable opens. The question now is, "What is actually going on with the debts?" Although we do not know what the original actions were, it is the central actions of the steward that might be seen in a different light.

Although we do not know the complete social and religious context of the story, or the nationalities of those involved, it is usually assumed that the characters are all Jews. In order to understand the steward's central actions, we must consider the legalities of usury or "interest" at that time. It is well known that the Judaism of the period forbade usury or lending at interest. Deuteronomy 23:19–20 states, "You shall not lend upon interest to your brother . . . to a foreigner you may lend upon interest . . ." (cf. Ex. 22:25–27; Lev. 25:35–37; Deut. 15:7–11; 24:10–13; 2 Kings 4:1–3; Neh. 5:4, 11; Ps. 15:5; Prov. 28:8; Ezek. 18:8, 13, 17; Hab. 2:6f.). However, in spite of strict laws against usury, it was still often entered into and the laws were flouted. Although it is of course possible that the master himself had entered into usury arrangements, this seems unlikely and it is more probable that the steward himself had done so. If he had, then when he changes the figures owed by the debtors (vv. 5–7), he is not simply reducing the amounts in order to make friends, nor is he giving away money that belongs to his master. Rather, he is relinquishing the interest he himself would have earned on the original amounts. In this case, the steward would not be doing his master out of any interest but would be losing money himself, and it would then make perfect sense if the master commended him for his actions. Of course, if the master had authorized the usury, which is still possible, then the reduced amounts would be a loss to him. It is also possible that the master might commend the steward for acting wisely with money even though he himself had lost out: as usury was forbidden among Jews, the reductions of the amounts were actually thoroughly just before God, and if the master commended the steward it was because he acted justly and showed prudence, skill, and foresight in a difficult situation. However, it seems more likely that the steward was the one who had entered into usury arrangements and that it was he who lost out in the reductions. Thus, even though the steward's original actions might have been unjust (indeed he is called unjust [*adikias*] in the parable itself), these are not the center of concern here. He is commended because of his prudence in dealing with the money in his central actions.

However, an important question to be answered here is, "Who is the person who commends the steward?" We are told in verse 8a that the "lord" commended the unjust steward for his prudence. But who is this "lord"? Is it the lord or master of the parable for whom the steward works? He has already been referred to as "lord" at verses 3 and 5, and other characters in Luke's parables are also referred to as "the lord" (cf. 12:37, 42b; 14:23). Or, is the lord of verse 8a Jesus the Lord, who is referred to as such frequently throughout Luke's Gospel? The question of which lord commends the steward reflects back to the problem of what he was doing and on what grounds he was commended. Those who have claimed that it is unlikely that the lord of the parable would have commended a steward who gave his master's money away argue that the Lord of verse 8 is Jesus. Jesus is called Lord at 18:6 and on seventeen other occasions in the Gospel, so it would be quite natural for "lord" to mean Jesus here. If this is the case, then verse 8a is Jesus' comment on the story of the steward. In either case, the commendation is odd if the steward is unjust in his central actions, unless he is simply commended for his prudence, which has been the usual view. But the problem of the identity of the lord in verse 8a raises the further question as to where the parable actually ends. Obviously if the "lord" here is the master of the parable then the parable ends with verse 8a. If he is Jesus, then it has already ended in verse 7. If the saying in verse 8b is part of the saying of the *kurios* and he is the master of the parable, then the parable ends at verse 8b. In fact, the view that the lord is the master of the parable can be supported by arguments from the text itself because if Jesus is the lord, then the parable seems to have no proper ending. The identity of the lord here remains ultimately unclear, but literary considerations favor the view that the lord is the rich man or master of the parable. Once again, if he commends the steward for his actions, it seems likely that he is not losing out and that the steward himself is the one who is prudent in losing out himself in order to gain later.

In the light of these basic historical and literary issues, we might now ask, "What is the real point of the parable?" or "What is its *crux interpretationis*?" Two questions focus the issues here: "Is the steward just or unjust?" And, "Is he an example of how to behave or how not to behave?" As we have already seen, the steward may not be unjust in his central actions. He is commended because he is *phronimos* in some way, i.e., sensible, prudent, or wise, a quality often associated with stewards (cf. 1 Cor. 4:1, 10; Matt. 25:2). The steward had acted prudently in some way in a crisis, and whether he acted justly or unjustly might be irrelevant. Here, we are back with the traditional interpretation.

But there is another possibility which leads us to our second question. This is that the word *phronimos* is to be understood ironically. In this view the steward is an example of how *not* to behave. He is an example to be avoided (cf. Paul's use of *phronimoi* at 1 Cor. 4:10; 2 Cor. 11:19; Rom. 11:25; and 12:16). In other words, the argument here is "Go and do what the steward did and see where it gets you!" The advantage of this view is that it does not really matter who commends the steward or whether he is just or unjust! However, there are those who say that the main thrust of this parable has to do with money and wealth rather than prudence. Along with poverty, wealth is certainly one of Luke's main concerns in his Gospel. Perhaps the message in the parable, then, is about giving away alms. It could be that in giving away money, the steward is performing an action pleasing to God, even if it is not his own. There are a number of occasions in Luke's parables when a bad or immoral character is used as an example: e.g., the Reluctant Friend (11:5–10); the Prodigal Son (15:11–32); and the Unjust Judge (18:2–14). Here the point is to urge the rich to give away their money. In response to this, however, it can be replied that even if wealth is a key theme, the steward has acted prudently with wealth, and in that case prudence is the overriding theme.

When we turn to the second section of the text, that is, verses 8b-13, we find a similar string of problems all of which are related, perhaps loosely, to the major issues in verses 1–8a. The second part of the text consists of several sayings concerning money and wealth and relating to the first part of the text in some way. There have been various views about how the sayings relate to the main story: some commentators have claimed that the sayings come from the same author, while others have been equally clear that they are a set of additions. In any case, the combining theme of the sayings is clearly "mammon" or money. Verse 9 is complex and bears back on the steward's central action. It seems to be an exhortation to make friends by using "unrighteous mammon." However, depending on what we think the crux of the parable is, the real thrust here could be "act wisely with money" (which is unrighteous stuff!) rather than "acquire money fraudulently" (or unrighteously). It is not altogether clear who will receive people into the eternal habitations (*aionious skenas*) or even what these are. It seems that they are not the usual temporary dwelling place meant by *skene* (cf. 4 Ezra 2:11; 1 Enoch 39:4; John 1:14), but a more permanent place. Both the receivers and the dwelling places are obviously in the realms of God and are to be contrasted with the realm of mammon. It seems that the "they" who will receive people could be: "angels," used as a circumlocution for God; or those who receive the alms; or the alms themselves personified. However, even if wealth is a major element in the concern of verse 9, it still seems that prudence is an overarching concern. In verses 10–13, which are attached more loosely to the parable, the main themes are faithfulness, dishonesty, and mammon. Faith (*pistis*) is commonly associated with stewards (cf. Luke 12:42; 19:17; 1 Cor. 4:2) and is contrasted here with unrighteous mammon. Verse 13 provides a dramatic climax to the whole passage with its message about God and mammon. Unlike verses 10–12, verse 13 is shared with Matthew (6:24), although Luke has added the word *oiketes* here, meaning a servant, probably to give a verbal link with his setting of the steward (*oikonomon*) (cf. Acts 10:17; Rom. 14:4; 1 Peter 2:18; Thomas 47). Depending on what view one takes of the relation of these sayings to the parable and of the meaning of the parable itself, it could be that this verse is somehow a summary of the meaning of the parable, although there seems to be at least a change of emphasis. Overall, the impression is that if the main interest of verses 1–8a is first prudence and then money, that interest is inverted in the sayings in verses 8b-13: wealth is now the primary concern, then prudence and faithfulness.

Two further observations of a literary sort support the view that the steward in this parable is prudent rather than unjust. First, many New Testament texts are, of course, directly related in one way or another to texts in the Hebrew Bible. It has been suggested that Luke may have had specific texts in mind as he incorporated this parable into his overall scheme. Some commentators have thought that some stories from 2 Kings might form the background. One is 2 Kings 7, which relates that during the siege of Samaria by Ben-hadad King of Syria, four lepers who were at the city gate went into the city rather than just sit and die. The crux of this story might be "act quickly and wisely in a crisis." Others have drawn attention to 2 Kings 13 and 14 as a possible background. The point here would be the same: during the reigns of Jehoahaz, Jehoash II, Jeroboam II, and Amaziah, prudent action was needed at a time of crisis.

Second, and more important, the position of our parable in Luke's literary scheme may also be able to tell us something. Luke 16:1–13 falls well within the central travel section of Luke

9:51–19:44, which Luke has inserted into the material he has taken over from Mark. Another literary section discernible between 14:25 and 17:11 is concerned with the use of wealth and of prudence in difficult situations. Within that, chapters 15 and 16 are concerned with a number of related themes that are woven together: the lost, money, and wealth. If we consider 16:1–13 within these concentric circles, the emphasis on prudence and money certainly fits in. Finally, the idea of turning a situation completely upside down is totally in line with the wider "reversal theology" of Luke's Gospel, and the steward's prudence as he faces a crisis, whether he is just or not, can certainly be seen in that light.

The so-called Parable of the Unjust Steward presents a kaleidoscope of interpretative problems for readers and scholars. Indeed, it is something of a New Testament exegete's paradise! Basically, a narrative concerning a steward's prudent action in a crisis is followed by a string of sayings concerning faithfulness and wealth. Every verse presents a number of different possible interpretations, and the verses and problems are intertwined sometimes to the point of paralyzing confusion. However, one of the great riches of the synoptic parables is that they do offer the possibility of different angles of interpretation and meaning. The notion of searching for a "single point" in parable interpretation was one of the ideals of German Protestant exegesis in the nineteenth century, and this is rapidly declining today. Rather, it is now understood that polyvalence or "multiple meanings" in the parables is a fundamental part of their nature. However, even though the parable in Luke 16 may mean different things to different audiences and different angles on the text might yield different insights, there is nevertheless the sense that when considered in his historical context, the steward in this parable may not have been unjust at all in his central actions. The Revised Standard Version of the Bible calls him the "dishonest steward," which one might well claim on the grounds of his original behavior leading to his dismissal. However, if that behavior is supposed to be the crux of the parable and dishonesty the central meaning, it is strange that we hear nothing specifically about what he did in the first place. Rather, it seems that whether the steward was just or unjust, honest or dishonest, he was at least acting shrewdly, wisely, or prudently with money in the crisis situation in which he found himself. It seems, therefore, that the real purpose of the story in Luke's Gospel is to exhort the disciples and readers to act quickly and prudently in difficult situations, especially when the time is short. It is wholly appropriate, therefore, that the central character in this story be called the Prudent Steward, and that the parable itself be known as the parable of the Prudent Steward.

EIGHT

STILLING THE STORM

CREATION, DISCIPLESHIP, AND DEMONS IN MARK 4:35–41 AND PARALLELS

The story of Jesus stilling a storm from a boat on the Sea of Galilee comprises one of the most dramatic events of the Gospel tradition (Mark 4:35–41 // Matt. 8:23–27 // Luke 8:22–25). Jesus is asleep in a boat on the sea. His panicking disciples wake him in fear as a storm rises and waves crash into the boat. With supreme confidence in God, he calms the storm and asks the disciples where their faith is. In amazement they ask, "Who is this, that even the wind and sea obey him?" The story, painted so effectively by Rembrandt in the seventeenth century, displays a vivid and engaging realism. The event is at once ordinary and extraordinary, natural and supernatural, revelatory and enigmatic. Within the tight fabric of the Gospel narrative, a tapestry of theological themes is woven in this story, revealing how creation, christology, eschatology, faith and discipleship, and the defeat of evil and chaos are all fundamentally intertwined.

In modern Western biblical exegesis and theology, the story of the stilling of the storm has often been thought of predominantly as a "nature miracle" whose central action is a "violation of the laws of nature." Its true theological richness, however, has frequently been obscured by this interpretation and much of its original symbolism has been missed. In this chapter, I first discuss the nature of the so-called Gospel "miracles"; second, I consider relevant symbolism in background ancient Near-Eastern creation myths and in the Hebrew Bible; and third, I offer an exegesis of the passage in Mark and its parallels in Matthew and Luke.

Miracles in the Gospel Tradition

A number of stories in the Gospels are popularly known as miracles, and before going any further, it is worth noting the key New Testament miracle material, beginning with Mark's Gospel. In Mark, Jesus is presented very quickly as a teacher and healer. He is often said to teach "in word and deed." His parables are then seen as the bedrock of his teaching in word, while his miracles are his teaching in deed. The miracle stories are then usually divided into healing miracles in which Jesus heals human sickness, and nature miracles in which he controls nature in some way. In Mark, there are generally reckoned to be eighteen miracles in all: thirteen healing miracles, and five nature miracles. The story of the stilling of the storm is obviously a nature miracle, although, as we shall see, it is also appropriate to see it as an exorcism and therefore possibly as a healing story. The stilling of the storm in Mark 4 follows Jesus' teaching in parables. This is then followed by another exorcism or healing story, that of the Gerasene Demoniac in chapter 5.

Matthew takes over most of Mark's miracle stories and has none peculiar to his own Gospel. Luke has his own additional miracle stories. Matthew and Luke together ("Q") share one miracle in common, that of the healing of the centurion's son. In the Fourth Gospel, the miracles stories are actually called "signs" by the author and the number is widely debated.

In fact, the word "miracle" as it has come to be understood in modern Western culture is rather misleading in relation to all of these stories and represents very little of the theological intention of the original authors. In short, the word "miracle" as it is widely understood today has no parallel in the Greek New Testament. Even the Latin word *miraculum* from which the English word comes actually means simply "an object of wonder." However, the word "miracle" in English has been interpreted largely in the manner associated with the Scottish Enlightenment philosopher David Hume: it is "a violation of the laws of nature." This notion of miracles was rooted in the cosmology associated with Isaac Newton, which saw the universe as a closed system of natural laws, a machine somewhat analogous to a clock that ticked along with complete regularity and predictability. It was a view of the universe as a machine in which no new or unlikely things could ever occur. Any activity of God in creation in this system was thought of as an intervention into these mechanistic "laws of nature."

Today this cosmology is still very powerful at the popular level, although it has begun to give way in some areas to ideas of a more flexible universe. For some of those working in the sciences the inadequacies of the Newtonian cosmology had already become clear through the scientific revolution associated with Albert Einstein. They have become even clearer more recently in the light of quantum and postmodern physics and our increasing knowledge about the human brain. The biblical cosmology itself was actually closer to some of these more recent cosmologies than it ever was to that of Newton. For inhabitants of the biblical world the universe was a fundamentally open and dynamic place in which novel things could occur especially through the activity of God. Of course, miracle workers were rife in the Jewish, Greek, and Roman worlds (the Greek "divine man" or *theios aner* tradition especially comes to mind here) and their miraculous deeds certainly include things that look contrary to nature, especially from a modern perspective. In the ancient world, however, the deeds of such people would have been seen primarily as vehicles of revelation or powerful acts of a god, rather than as "violations of the laws of nature." The ancients obviously did not perceive the cosmos in terms of

Newtonian physics. A full understanding of the Gospel "miracle" stories can only emerge, then, when the open, dynamic cosmology of the original authors is taken into account.

In the original language of the synoptic Gospels, the word used of the familiar "miracle stories" is not the Latin *miraculum* but the Greek *dunamis*, that is, a "work of mighty power." The word *dunamis* has much more of the sense of a "revelatory event" than of a "violation of the laws of nature." It is interesting that in the Fourth Gospel the word used for Jesus' miracles is *semeia* or "signs." In the theology of the fourth evangelist the meaning of *semeia* is actually quite close to the synoptic *dunamis*: it is an event in which God is revealed. In all of these so-called "miracle stories," then, the New Testament writers were not focusing on the idea that the "laws of nature" had been broken by Jesus, or that God had intervened into an otherwise totally closed and predictable mechanistic natural system. Rather, for them the miracle stories of the Gospel tradition were stories about the revelation of God in creation. It is in this light that the story of the stilling of the storm is best approached.

Stilling the Storm: Creation, Eschatology, and Demons

Although popularly interpreted on the basis of Newtonian cosmology, reading the narratives of Jesus' works of mighty power in this way is obviously misleading. The contemporary worldview of the original writers must be taken into account if the story is to be allowed its full impact. Indeed, aspects of the cosmology of the ancient Near East turn out to be particularly enlightening when it comes to the stilling of the storm story. What symbolism would have been in play for the original readers or hearers of this story? And what understanding of creation stands behind the story?

The first thing to note is that the setting of the Gospel story of the stilling of the storm is the sea: the event takes place on the sea. This feature alone is of exceptional symbolic significance. In the Hebrew Bible, the sea is particularly associated with the waters of creation and with the great dragons of the deep, Leviathan, Rahab, and Behemoth. Some of the greatest events of the Hebrew Bible involve the sea: the waters of Genesis; the Red Sea of the Exodus; and Jonah and the big fish. These all stand in the background of any story in the New Testament that is set on the sea.

Furthermore, the sea and the dragons of the deep played a key role in a number of older creation myths of the ancient Near East. Three traditions especially come to mind: the Babylonian *Epic of Gilgamesh*, dating from sometime in the third millennium BCE; the Babylonian text known by its opening words *Enuma Elish*, dating from about the fourteenth century BCE; and the texts from Ugarit (Ras Shamra) also dating from about the fourteenth century BCE. The creation myths found in these texts and traditions all associate the processes of creation with the sea. Let us look at them more closely.

The *Epic of Gilgamesh* concerns Gilgamesh, the King of Uruk whose friend Enkidu dies. Gilgamesh becomes aware of his own mortality and begins the search for eternal life. He visits Utnapishtim who tells him of his experiences in a great flood. He tells Gilgamesh that he was commanded in a dream to destroy his house and build a ship with the wood. He built the ship and put types of every animal into it. He then got into the ship and a mighty flood came. Thunder, lightning, and raging sea tossed the ship, which became an ark of salvation. Utnapishtim sent out a dove and then a swallow, both of which returned. He then sent out a raven which did not. The storm was then over. By the end of the story, Gilgamesh has learned that Utnapishtim has achieved eternal life by surviving the deluge. The ship has carried him to safety and he has become like the gods. Obviously this story is closely related in substance to the story of Noah's Ark in Genesis 6–9 and was for a long time thought to have influenced it.

The second tradition, *Enuma Elish*, takes its name from the opening words of the text "when above." The opening lines refer to a time when the heaven above was not yet created. The poem is a creation epic that begins with the waters of pre-creation. The god Marduk competes with his opponent Tiamat, who has created an army of monsters. There is a cosmic struggle; Marduk kills Tiamat and splits her body apart. With one half he makes the sky, with the other the earth, and the creation is complete.

The third tradition, the one from Ugarit, is in many ways the most important for us here, even though it is not a creation myth as such. It is, rather, a series of texts that refer to the struggle between Baal and the sea god Yam. Yam is destroyed and Baal is established as king. It is these Ugaritic texts that are now thought to lie behind the many references in the Hebrew Bible to the sea and the dragons called Leviathan, Rahab, and Behemoth. Of course, we cannot say that these texts and traditions have directly influenced the later texts of the Hebrew Bible, but along with the biblical texts they display a common cosmological outlook in which water, chaos, and a struggle with a monster or dragon leads to the defeat of evil and the establishment of order in creation.

It is worth noting just how frequently some of these basic themes occur in the Hebrew Bible, especially in the Psalms. God controls the waters of creation and defeats the dragons of the sea: e.g., "Thou didst divide the sea by thy might; thou didst break the heads of the dragons on the waters. / Thou didst crush the heads of Leviathan . . ." (Ps. 74:13–14; cf. 33:7; 65:7; 89:9–10; 93:3–4; 104:6–7). In terms of the stilling of the storm story in the Gospels, the following is particularly relevant: "Then they cried to the Lord in their trouble, and he delivered them from their distress; / he made the storm be still, and the waves of the sea were hushed. / Then they were glad because they had quiet, and he brought them to their desired haven" (107:28–29). Some of these fundamental themes appear also in the book of Job (e.g., Job 3:8; 7:12; 9:8–13; 26:5–14; 38:8–11) and in the prophetic literature (e.g., Is. 17:12–13; 27:1; Hab. 3:8–10). In a number of texts the use of the sea and dragon imagery is attached to specific nations that surround Israel and come to symbolize hostility, horror, or evil: for example, Egypt is called Rahab (Is. 30:7; cf. Ezek. 29:3; 32:2; Jer. 51:34). The sea, dragon, and conflict imagery, however, is not only associated with creation, but also with God's purposes at the end of time. The imagery is also, therefore, eschatological and apocalyptic. In the Book of Daniel four beasts come up out of the sea (Dan. 7:3); the ancient of days appears and in the ensuing conflict the fourth "terrible and dreadful" beast (7:7) is defeated and his body destroyed (v. 11). At this point "one like a son of man" appears and is "given dominion and glory and kingdom" (7:13). As might be expected, the apocalyptic, eschatological use of the imagery of the sea and of beasts and dragons also occurs in the New Testament book of Revelation: "a great red dragon, with seven heads and ten horns . . ." (12:3); the beast that arises out of the sea (13:1); and finally in the great vision of the new heaven and earth, the sea is no more (21:1). The sea is not only associated with the creation, then, but also with the end of time and the elimination of evil, chaos, and conflict.

The creation myths of the ancient Near East, the *Epic of Gilgamesh*, *Enuma Elish*, and the traditions from Ugarit, in addition to texts of the Hebrew Bible, especially the Psalms, share a common cosmology in which the sea is a symbol of pre-creation chaos; its dragons are symbols of chaos and evil; and the defeat of the dragons and the control of the sea show the power of the creator god concerned. Setting a story on the sea automatically draws on traditions in which a god acts dramatically in creation so that order might be brought out of chaos. Such a setting evokes a theology of creation, eschatology, and the defeat of demons. For the very first Christians, the texts of the Hebrew Bible and the cosmology that pervades them were foundational to understanding God and the world. Hearing a story about Jesus in a boat on the sea would automatically evoke certain meanings and associations and would have been understood as primarily about God's activity in creation. How, more particularly, then, do all these traditions bear on the synoptic story of the stilling of the storm?

Stilling the Storm: Creation, Demons, and Discipleship

The New Testament story of the stilling of the storm occurs in all three synoptic Gospels. It is not in John, although Jesus does walk on the water there (John 6:16–21 // Matt. 14:22–33 // Mark 6:45–52). Although the extent to which such narratives should be allegorized is debatable, the setting of all of them is the sea, bringing with it much of the symbolism we have noted in the previous section. I shall consider Mark's version of the stilling of the storm to be primary and Matthew to have edited it. Luke's version is very much like Mark's and has no new significant details. In Mark's Gospel the story appears in chapter 4, which consists mostly of parables. Jesus is already known as Son of God, a healer, and as one who teaches with authority (cf. 1:11, 21–28). The parables form a fundamental part of Jesus' teaching on the nature of the kingdom of God. In the early chapters of Mark, Jesus' words and deeds are both very much in the foreground. As we have already noted, the stilling of the storm is a "work of mighty power" or *dunamis*. Thus, after the parable of the mustard seed and a note about Jesus' teaching in parables from the author, the reader learns that on the same day in the evening Jesus initiates a trip across the sea. Jesus' teaching in parables has already been related to the sea in 4:1: he was teaching from a boat and a crowd was on the shore. Now in 4:35, he wishes to cross the sea. Here in Mark, the disciples then take him with them into the boat. Mark makes the comment that there are other boats with them on the sea. The setting of the sea and the boat here already evoke the creation myths of the ancient Near East and of Genesis. But it is also possible that the boat signifies the church, the new ark of salvation for Mark's community. This latter is certainly the way later Christians from the second century onwards saw the image of the boat, and Justin Martyr, Tertullian, and Hippolytus go further, seeing connections between the wood of the ark and the boat, and the wood of the cross of Jesus' crucifixion.

Next, a storm blows up and fills the boat with water. The symbolism of the destructive power of chaos is paramount. Jesus is "in the stern, asleep on the cushion" (v. 38). With a touch of vivid realism, Mark evokes an image from the Psalms: sleep is a sign of faith in God (cf. Ps. 3:5; Ps. 4:8). Jesus is depicted here as one who is at peace with God as the chaos of the storm mounts. The disciples awaken Jesus, and say "Teacher, do you not care if we perish?" (v. 38). In Greek the word is *didaskale*, "teacher," precisely the one who has been teaching them with authority in the parables. The language of perishing is powerful and evokes more than the possibility of physical harm or death. Jesus then wakes up and rebukes the wind and calms the sea.

The scene evokes many of the texts identified in the previous section, in which God controls the sea in the processes of creation—for example, "Thou dost rule the raging of the sea; when its waves rise, thou stillest them" (Ps. 89:9). Jesus' words here are particularly important in the Greek text, *siopa, pephimoso*, that is, "peace, be muzzled." The first word *siopa* means "peaceful," "silent," "dumb," "hushed," or "calm." The second word *pephimoso* comes from *phimoo*, which means "I muzzle." The "muzzling" here is obviously an image of control of the chaos. Jesus uses the same word here (*phimoo*) that he has already used to silence the demon in 1:25 in the synagogue in Capernaum. The demon inside the man is of the same sort as the demons in the sea.

Next, after calm has come to the sea, Jesus questions the disciples about their faith (*pistis*), that is, the total trust in God that he has himself exhibited in his sleep. Where is theirs? The order of the events in all this is significant. The story is primarily a "work of mighty power" in which Jesus controls the storm. It is then a story about the faith of the disciples, and of course about the nature of Jesus himself. The disciples, typically in Mark, are filled with awe and confusion as they ask, "Who is this that even the wind and the sea obey him?" This fundamental question turns out to be Jesus' main question to them in 8:27—"Who do people say that I am?"—and is the central christological question of the

Gospel. The answer to the disciples' question here is that this is Jesus, teacher, healer, and controller of the storm. He controls creation, defeats demons, and encourages faith and discipleship.

In Matthew's version of the story there are some interesting differences of detail, and the new focus is discipleship. For Matthew, of course, Jesus is just as much a teacher and a performer of works of mighty power as he is in Mark, and more so. And Mark himself had already emphasized discipleship. But the setting and structure of the story are now different in Matthew. The parables that Matthew has taken over from Mark 4 are in Matthew 13, and the storm narrative in Matthew now follows healings in Capernaum and material relating to discipleship. In Matthew 8:18–22, material on discipleship sets the scene: a scribe declares that he will follow Jesus wherever he goes, while a disciple who wants to bury his father before he follows Jesus is told, "Follow me, and leave the dead to bury their own dead" (8:22). The occurrence of the word follow (*akoloutheo*) and the theme of following link in with Matthew's wider interest in discipleship (cf. Matt. 5–7, the Sermon on the Mount). It is interesting that thereafter, it is the disciples who follow Jesus into the boat (unlike Mark, where they go first). The disciples' cry is "save us, Lord (*kurios*)," introducing specific themes of salvation and Jesus' Lordship. Jesus is now not only a "teacher" as in Mark, but more clearly the "Lord" controlling creation.

Also, the order of events in the story has changed: the disciples' faith is the first issue to arise when they question why Jesus isn't concerned that they're in danger. He refers to them as *oligopistoi* "having little faith." By this change, Matthew makes faith and discipleship more central than it had been in Mark. Only after introducing faith does Jesus calm the storm and the disciples marvel at who he is. Overall, Matthew's version has developed rather than changed Mark's text, giving it new thrusts of meaning while retaining the basic ones from Mark. Now, in Matthew, in addition to the sea imagery and Jesus as controller of creation, it is clear that

Jesus is Lord of creation and that faith in him and following him are an important part of that. Creation, eschatology, Jesus' Lordship, and the defeat of evil are all intertwined in the narrative. As in Mark, Matthew's stilling of the storm story is followed by that of the Gerasene Demoniac, recalling perhaps Ps. 65:7, ". . . who dost still the roaring of the seas, the roaring of their waves, the tumult of the peoples."

Finally, in Luke's version the setting is slightly different, although it is still preceded by teaching in parables, and followed by the Gerasene Demoniac. The order of events is the same as in Mark, although when the disciples speak to Jesus, Luke uses the Greek word *epistata* meaning "master," instead of *didaskalos*. The overall thrust of the story in Luke, however, remains substantially the same as that in Mark.

We have seen that the story of the stilling of the storm, like the other great "works of mighty power" performed by Jesus in the Gospels, should not primarily be understood as a "miracle" in the Enlightenment sense of Isaac Newton and David Hume. The original author of the text would not have seen this as a story about God intervening into a system of mechanistic laws and thereby breaking the laws of nature. Rather, the story must be approached from within the cosmology and symbolism that permeated the ancient Near East at the turn of the eras. Texts like the *Epic of Gilgamesh*, *Enuma Elish*, and those from Ugarit, as well as the great creation texts of the Hebrew Bible, display common themes that influenced this Gospel story. The notion of a god who acts in the waters of chaos, or the sea, in order to bring about order and defeat the dragons of the deep, permeates much of the literature of the ancient world.

When we read the synoptic stilling of the storm story, therefore, we can read it anew as a text that presents Jesus doing the work of God and bringing order out of chaos, defeating the demons and nurturing discipleship in those who believe. The story of the stilling of the storm is a combat story focusing on the defeat of chaos and the establishment of order in creation; not a nature miracle as often understood, but an exorcism or healing story. It draws upon a long tradition of creation myths, producing a rich tapestry that weaves fundamental themes of Christian theology into a single narrative form: creation, christology, eschatology, discipleship, and the defeat of chaos and evil. In the end, the story of the stilling the storm is about Jesus bringing order into creation, about him enabling creation to be what it should essentially be, rather than about him breaking the laws of nature.

NINE

METAMORPHOSIS

TRANSFIGURATION, SUFFERING, AND DEATH IN MARK 9:2–8 AND PARALLELS

The story of the transfiguration of Jesus lies at the heart of the synoptic Gospels. Following the crucial question of Jesus to his disciples at Caesarea Philippi, "Who do people say I am?" and the various responses, the transfiguration forms part of the christological "pivot" of the narratives of Matthew, Mark, and Luke (Mark 9:2–8 // Matt. 17:1–8 // Luke 9:28–36; cf. 2 Peter 1:16–18). Of course, the Fourth Gospel might also be said to be concerned with the transfiguration of Jesus with its emphasis on his suffering and glory, but the synoptic story itself is conspicuous by its absence there. For many commentators, the synoptic transfiguration story presents major interpretative difficulties: Is it a real historical event? Is it a mythical story with spiritual significance? Does the event imply a change in Jesus' awareness of God? Or is it a change in the disciples' perception of Jesus? Is it supposed to be seen as a foretaste of the resurrection, perhaps in origin a stray resurrection appearance story as Rudolph Bultmann famously suggested? Or is it a different type of event from the resurrection altogether?

In fact, the transfiguration narrative presents a kaleidoscope of literary and theological elements, all of which contribute to the significance of the story. The aim of this chapter is not to address all these questions, let alone answer them, but rather to focus on some major theological themes in the narratives, especially that of the relation between transfiguration and suffering and death. By way of approach, I first briefly draw attention to the rich legacy of the narrative of the transfiguration in iconography, art, and geography; second, I discuss the chapters of the Book of Exodus upon which the transfiguration story so heavily relies; and third, I offer detailed exegeses of the three synoptic accounts of the transfiguration. I shall not discuss 2 Peter 1:16–18, which in any case is briefer and theologically substantially the same as the synoptic accounts.

Iconography, Art, and Geography

The transfiguration of Jesus is not only a vivid narrative lying at the heart of the synoptic Gospels. From the second century onwards, it became a central element in Christian theological reflection and devotion. In turn, this gave rise to a rich tradition of Christian art and iconography, especially in the Eastern churches. Numerous stunning icons and mosaics in churches across the world feature the image of the transfigured Christ as a focus of liturgy and prayer. In the Greek, Russian, and other Orthodox traditions, the transfiguration has been a key subject for icon writers. At the heart of the Sinai Desert, for example, in the Greek Orthodox Monastery of St. Catherine, in the apse of the Church of the Transfiguration, a restored sixth-century mosaic features the transfiguration of Christ with the figures of Moses and Elijah and the disciples Peter, James, and John nearby. Its stark and vivid realism radiates out across the church and the desert, connecting Sinai and the ancient Jewish theology of covenant, promise, and Torah with the Christian theology of transfiguration.

Theologically, Mount Sinai is connected with Mount Tabor in Galilee where Christian pilgrims have marked the transfiguration of Jesus since the fourth century. In fact, in the early Christian centuries, several mountains came to be associated with the transfiguration: Mount Hermon in the north of Israel (situated close to Caesarea Philippi), a location that seemed to follow logically from the synoptic narratives; the Mount of Olives in Jerusalem, widely associated in Judaism and Christianity with the coming of God or the Messiah; and Mount Tabor in the Jezreel Valley in Galilee, which remains the focus today.

Far from being simply an important Gospel narrative, therefore, the transfiguration has featured significantly in the theology and devotion of Christians down the centuries and has given rise to a rich legacy of icons, mosaics, and geographical associations. In the Holy Land today, art and iconography join with geography and pilgrimage as part of the legacy of the transfiguration story. But what is it that is celebrated or remembered in this legacy? And what is the central theological message of the New Testament accounts? In order to answer these questions, we must turn first to the background of the story of the transfiguration in the Book of Exodus.

Background in Exodus

The roots of the synoptic accounts of the transfiguration are to be found in the material dealing with Moses' encounter with God at Sinai in Exodus 24 and 33–34 and in the narratives dealing with Elijah in 1 Kings 17–2 Kings 2:14. The Exodus narrative concerns the establishment of the covenant between Israel and God. Moses' encounter with God is symbolized by a cloud covering the mountain. The key Kings narrative is 1 Kings 19 and concerns Elijah fleeing from Queen Jezebel to Horeb or Sinai, and encountering God in the "still small voice." For both Moses and Elijah, the mountain in Sinai is the location of an overwhelming revelation of God; it is a place and an occasion of theophany. For obvious reasons, Moses eventually came to epitomize the Torah, while Elijah came to epitomize Israel's prophets. It is predominantly the theophany to Moses in Exodus that provides the literary and theological symbolism later taken up by the synoptic authors of the transfiguration narratives. A brief glance at some of the major themes from the Exodus narrative, therefore, will prepare the way for an exegesis of the transfiguration accounts themselves.

In Exodus 24 God summons Moses with his three companions to the mountain for the establishment of the covenant (v. 1f.). At the mountain, along with seventy elders of Israel, they "beheld God" (v. 11). Moses then ascends the mountain and a cloud, the *shekinah*, covers the mountain (v. 15). The cloud is a symbol in the Hebrew Bible for the overwhelming presence of God. The reader is then told that the glory (Hebrew: *kabod*; Greek: *doxa*) of God settled on the mountain, words that evoke the special shining presence of the divine. The cloud stays over the mountain for "six days," and on the seventh day God's voice calls from the cloud to Moses (v. 16). The event is clearly a theophany or revelation in which God appears to the group. It is an event establishing the covenant and the Torah and one that lies at the roots of Israel's very identity.

Exodus chapters 33–34 are also important in coming to appreciate the meaning of the transfiguration narratives. The text is multilayered, and it is only necessary here to note the significant details. On this occasion Moses is at the tent of meeting in the desert, and God speaks to him. A pillar of cloud (again, the *shekinah*) accompanies him. The presence of God is then specifically named (33:14). Moses asks to see God's glory (*kabod*; *doxa*), but God says that Moses will only be allowed to see his back. In Exodus 34 the event is the renewing of the covenant and the re-cutting of the tablets of the Torah. Again God appears in a cloud, and in the instructions that are given to Moses we read, "Six days you shall work, but on the seventh day you shall rest" (v. 21), indicating Sabbath rest in the context of a theophany. When Moses came down the mountain "the skin of his face shone because he had been talking with God" (v. 29), and he put on a veil. The shining of the face symbolizes the encounter with the glory of the divine presence. In all this, Moses comes to epitomize Israel's covenant, Torah, and Decalogue.

The authors of the synoptic transfiguration narratives have used much of the symbolism from this theophany as the basis of their accounts of the transfiguration of Jesus. In what ways do these symbols permeate the transfiguration narratives themselves? An exegesis of each text will make this clear.

The Synoptic Accounts of the Transfiguration

(a) Mark 9:2–8

Mark's account of the transfiguration of Jesus follows the event at Caesarea Philippi (8:27–33) which is so crucial to the structure, christology, and development of his Gospel. In the Caesarea Philippi narrative, one of the major themes is that of the suffering of the Son of Man, and in what is the first of the three great passion predictions in Mark, the reader learns that "the Son of Man must suffer many things" (8:31; cf. 9:31; 10:33; and 10:45). There is also the theme of the disciples taking up the cross (v. 34) and later the announcement of the coming of the kingdom of God with power (9:1). The transfiguration narrative is followed by material on secrecy and further material on the suffering of the Son of Man (vv. 9–13) and then the healing of the epileptic boy (9:14–29). The account of the transfiguration, therefore, is surrounded by material on christology, suffering, and healing. The connection between the suffering Son of Man and the transfiguration is often overlooked but is actually central to the overall message about Jesus in this Gospel.

When the transfiguration narrative itself opens in 9:2, Mark makes an immediate link with Exodus 24:16 by beginning "after six days." In Exodus 24 the cloud of God's presence had covered the mountain for six days and on the seventh day God spoke out of the cloud. In Exodus 34:21, six days of work and a seventh day of rest evoke the Genesis creation narrative. Thus, Mark's setting evokes the theophany of the Exodus mountain and the perfection of Sabbath rest. Jesus leads the way up the mountain, taking with him the three disciples of the "inner group," Peter, James, and John, so well known in Mark (cf. 5:37; 13:3; 14:33). In Exodus 24:1, Moses had three companions with him. The transfiguration mountain itself evokes the theophany at Sinai, the establishment of the covenant, and the giving of the Torah and Decalogue. Mark uses the Greek word *metamorphoo* of the central event here, indicating a change of "form" (*morphe*) in Jesus' appearance. Jesus' garments glisten with whiteness, and the reference to an earthly fuller or soap reminds the reader of the shining of Moses' face on the mountain in Exodus 34. The glistening is also an apocalyptic symbol indicating theophany and revelation. Paul had already used this Exodus story in 2 Corinthians 3:12–18, and he might well have influenced Mark.

Next, Elijah and Moses appear, signifying the prophets and the Torah. As we have seen, both were associated with Sinai or Horeb; both were also associated with the end of time, and there were expectations of their return. Mark's comment that Elijah and Moses "were talking to Jesus" perhaps indicates dialogue between Judaism as it had been and the emerging faith of the Christians with their new perception of God in Jesus. In any case, by the end of the event, Jesus has superseded them and is the only one left (v. 8). In verse 5 Peter suggests building three booths. He refers to Jesus as *rabbi*, picking up the powerful theme in Mark of Jesus the teacher (9:5; cf. 1:22; 4:38; 10:51; 11:21; 14:45). Jesus is portrayed as standing in line with Elijah and Moses. The booths or tabernacles (Hebrew: *succoth*) come from the wilderness wandering period (Lev. 23:39–43; Neh. 8:13–18) and are part of the journey of the people into the land of Israel. Mark then comments on the disciples' fear, another major theme of this Gospel (4:40; 6:50; 9:32; 16:8). In verse 7 a cloud, the *shekinah* of Exodus 24 and 33, signifying the presence of God, overshadows them (cf. Ex. 16:10; 19:9; 24:15–18; 33:9–11). As in Exodus 24:16, a voice comes from the cloud; it is the *bat qol* or "daughter of the voice," an echo of God's own voice. It recalls the voice at Jesus' baptism which tells Jesus, "You are my son" (1:11). Now, in 9:7 it is a general announcement to all those present: "This is my son." In any case, baptism and transfiguration are both definitive moments in Jesus' ministry and in his journey to the cross. After the voice, the reader learns that Elijah and Moses have gone; only Jesus remains with the disciples. Clearly, Jesus has fulfilled or superseded the prophets and the Torah. In 9:9 the major themes of secrecy and of the suffering and rising of the Son of Man occur again, and the cross is more clearly in sight than ever. The full significance of the transfiguration is to be found in the suffering of the Son of Man on his way to the cross.

(b) Matthew 17:1–8

Matthew's account of the transfiguration is essentially the same as Mark's, although there are some significant differences. Matthew's transfiguration, like Mark's, follows his Caesarea Philippi narrative with its material on the suffering of the Son of Man (16:13–28) and is itself followed by the healing of an afflicted boy (17:14–20). Suffering is central once again and is intertwined with transfiguration. As usual, Matthew has a tidier version of the story than Mark: he has sharpened Mark's Greek style, and the typical roughness of Mark's narrative is cleaned up by changing some details in keeping with Matthew's theology throughout his Gospel. For a start, Matthew makes a new comment about the actual transfiguration: Jesus' "face shone like the sun" and his garments are "white as light" (cf. Dan. 12:3; 4 Ezra 7:97; 2 Cor. 3:7, 13). There is a stronger apocalyptic tone here, although Mark's detail about bleach is omitted.

More importantly, in Matthew, Peter addresses Jesus as "Lord" (*kurios*) instead of Master (*rabbi*) as in Mark, which heightens the christological content of the passage. The shift is indicative of Matthew's firmer theological and ecclesiological stance, perhaps reflecting a later stage in the development of the tradition: Jesus is now firmly "Lord" (cf. Mark 4:38 // Matt. 8:25). In Matthew, Peter adds, deferentially, "if you wish" before his suggestion that they build three booths. Matthew adds that the cloud overshadowing them is "bright," thus providing a sharper picture (as with Jesus' shining face). The words of the voice from the cloud now include "with whom I am well pleased," linking it back to Matthew's baptism scene (3:13–17). Matthew retains Mark's "listen to him." In Matthew 17:6, in new Matthean material, the disciples fall on their faces and are filled with awe, and Jesus says "Rise, and have no fear." Again, there is a touch of Matthean apocalyptic drama here reminiscent of his resurrection scene where the guards fall down as if dead (28:1–10). The final comment in Matthew's transfiguration scene provides a clearer focus on Jesus as the one who supersedes Elijah and Moses (v. 8). Once again, as in Mark, the context and the content underline the link between the suffering of the Son of Man on his way to the cross and his transfiguration.

(c) Luke 9:28–36

Luke's account of the transfiguration story contains some new material and some interesting developments. Overall there is a more polished and less enigmatic feel than in Mark's version. The narrative has the same general context as that in the other Gospels: it follows Jesus' question to his disciples about his identity (9:18–22), although Luke does not name the place as Caesarea Philippi. Significantly, Luke has material on taking up the cross, and on saving life and losing it, now linked slightly differently to the Son of Man (vv. 23–27). As in Mark and Matthew, Luke's narrative is followed by the story of the afflicted boy (vv. 37–43).

Luke's transfiguration narrative itself opens rather differently from that of Mark and Matthew: he has "about eight days after these sayings." The eight days have often been thought to signify the beginning of a new week and hence of a new creation. However, "about eight" could easily be seven and, therefore, essentially the same as "after six"! Luke changes the order of the names of the disciples, now "Peter and John and James" (cf. 8:51). More important, the setting for Luke is one of Jesus at prayer, a major Lukan interest that appears elsewhere, and is sometimes added to Markan material that Luke has taken over and edited (cf. 3:21; 5:16; 6:12; 9:18; 11:1; 22:32, 44). The occasion of the transfiguration in Luke is thus one on which Jesus is in the close presence of God. Luke's language for the central event is different from that in the other accounts: "his countenance was altered" (v. 29). The impact is lessened, perhaps, at the side of Mark and Matthew, but Jesus' clothes are now dazzling white. As in Matthew, there is no reference to the Markan bleach.

The next section of Luke's narrative is extended at the side of the other Gospels. Luke says "two men" appeared. They are reminiscent of the two men in the resurrection and ascension narratives (24:4; Acts 1:10). Moses and Elijah appear "in glory" (*en doxe*). This *doxa* indicates the radical presence of God and is closely aligned with the cloud that appears later on. The *doxa* here is also that referred to in Exodus 33. The glory gives a more secure status to Moses and Elijah here. Even though, as in the other accounts, they have disappeared completely by the end, they nevertheless have a heavenly or quasi-angelic status. It is as though Jesus has glorified them retrospectively and their place is still significant. This is well in keeping with Luke's wider attitude to the Jewish past in Luke-Acts. A conversation between Moses, Elijah, and Jesus concerns Jesus' *exodus* (v. 31). Luke's use of this word obviously evokes the events of the book of Exodus, but also links Jesus' own journey and death to that of the people of Israel on their way to the land of Israel. In Luke, the central "journey" section of the Gospel (9:51–19:44), including Jesus' journey to the cross, is just about to begin.

Luke's specific mention of Jerusalem at 9:31 is important not only as a reference to the cross and resurrection and the journey toward it, but also as a key Lukan theme. Jerusalem and the temple play a central role in Luke's narrative, constantly pulling events toward that powerful center of revelation, the city where God's presence had been made known through history in Judaism and was now being made known anew in Jesus. It is this city in which Luke opens his Gospel with a theophany to Zechariah in the temple, and which is to feature regularly thereafter (cf. 1:9; 2:22f., 41f.; 9:51; 13:34; 17:11; 18:31; 19:28). Significantly, the resurrection appearances in Luke are not in Galilee, as in the other Gospels, but in Jerusalem and the region of Jerusalem (24:13, 33, 53). The city is thus the location of the events of God's saving history, now being worked out in the events of Jesus' life and death. The mention of Jerusalem here therefore evokes revelation and the coming suffering and death of the Son of Man, followed by his resurrection.

In verse 32, the disciples are "heavy with sleep." This is reminiscent of Gethsemane (22:45), although they actually stay awake here and see Jesus' *doxa* which now aligns him with God, as in Exodus 33. In a striking comment, Luke refers to Moses and Elijah departing as they speak with Jesus. There is a sense here that the whole scene and the ensuing journey are part of the process of Moses and Elijah diminishing in significance, even though they have been "glorified" by the events that have taken place. Peter now asks his question about the booths, addressing Jesus with a word that does not occur in Mark and Matthew, *epistata*, meaning essentially "master" but with a heightened element of respect for the authority of the one of whom it is used (cf. 5:5; 8:24, 45; 9:33, 49; 17:13). Luke's comment that Peter didn't know what he said is similar to Mark but not Matthew. The element of confusion arises from the overwhelming nature of the event, although Luke moves the Markan fear forward.

At this point in Luke, the cloud or *shekinah* appears and then there is fear; the voice from the cloud is essentially the same as in

Mark. The disciples' fear is associated specifically with the presence of God indicated by the cloud. Luke's ending is clearer than Mark's and much more like Matthew's: Jesus is the only one there by the end. There is no "looking around" as in Mark. Luke adds "silence" at the end, reminiscent of much in Mark's theological scheme.

Overall, the Lukan account is somewhat extended at the side of the others. Some of Luke's key themes, such as prayer and Jerusalem, appear. He also makes more of the connection with the exodus. At the side of Mark and Matthew, the overall emphasis on suffering is perhaps slightly diminished, as it is in Luke's overall christology, but still present, nevertheless, as the journey to Jerusalem and the cross begins.

What, then, is the central message of the synoptic accounts of the transfiguration of Jesus? And why did this event in the Gospel narratives become so important in later iconography, art, and pilgrimage? First, it is clear that the three accounts are built substantially out of Exodus 24 and 33–34. This indicates immediately that the synoptic authors saw the transfiguration of Jesus primarily as a theophany. It is a revelation of God, but now in Jesus. Many of the symbols in the transfiguration accounts are clearly taken directly from the imagery of this theophany to Moses: the exodus; the six days; the mountain; the three companions; the cloud; the shining face; and the voice. In Exodus and in the Gospels, the occasion is one on which the presence and glory of God are made known.

But the synoptic writers make an additional theological point. The context in which the narrative appears is one that emphasizes the suffering of the Son of Man on his journey to the cross. By mentioning this suffering before and after the transfiguration, the writers draw attention to the fact that the sort of glory the Son of Man will have is one that passes along the way of suffering, through to death. A significantly different theology is at play here from that in Exodus, for although there was suffering in the arduous journeys the Israelites made toward the Promised Land, in Jesus glory is now substantially intertwined with suffering. With this, the christology of the Fourth Gospel comes once again to mind, for there the death of the suffering Son of Man, more than his resurrection, is the focus of glory and the point of accomplishment of his purpose (cf. John 19:30). Similarly, the synoptic accounts of the transfiguration provide a glimpse of the combination of suffering, death, and glory that will later constitute the resurrection. The transfiguration story, therefore, is not a resurrection narrative gone astray, but a prior glimpse of the way in which suffering and glory, death and resurrection combine in God's overall purposes in Jesus. The transfiguration is a first insight into what will be played out more completely later in the death and resurrection themselves. The power of this insight fed the Christian imagination very early on, and there is no wonder that generations of artists tried to capture something of its essence in their icons and mosaics, or that it became such a potent focus of pilgrimage and devotion.

TEN

RESURRECTION
THE SPIRITUAL BODY IN 1 CORINTHIANS AND THE GOSPELS

Most people would agree that the resurrection of Jesus of Nazareth from the dead lies at the heart of the Christian faith. Take away the resurrection, they would argue, and the Christian faith disappears. After all, didn't St. Paul write to the Corinthians that if Christ had not been raised then their faith was in vain? Surely the resurrection of Jesus is of the very essence of the Christian faith. Of course, there are theologians who might stress the incarnation more than the resurrection, but few would deny the resurrection a place at the center of Christianity. The usual point of Christian disagreement about the resurrection of Jesus is over exactly how to interpret it.

In contemporary Western debates the focus is often on whether or not it ever really happened historically or whether it is a mythical story carrying a spiritual or existential meaning. Implicit in such debates are issues about whether the dead do ever rise; whether "miracles" such as a resurrection can ever happen; and whether God intervenes in creation and history to bring such things about in the first place. In many of these debates the New Testament material on the resurrection often remains unclear, and the different accounts of the writers simply add to the confusion. Even where the New Testament material does enter the discussion, an important strand is still sometimes overlooked: it concerns the nature of Jesus' resurrection body. In this chapter I first draw attention to some background texts and concepts; and then second, I offer brief exegetical studies of the New Testament resurrection material in Paul and the four Gospels.

Background

A thoroughly comprehensive study of the resurrection of Jesus would include an enormous amount of background material. Questions about the nature of space and time, life and death, epistemology and perception would all need to feature. Some of these themes will surface here from time to time insofar as they arise in this study of the material in 1 Corinthians 15 and the New Testament Gospels. Before we begin, however, it is important to ask what people believed about resurrection in the centuries leading up to the time of Jesus. Was there a common philosophy or understanding of resurrection which the first Christians took over?

It is widely known that the Hebrew Bible and ancient Judaism have little or nothing to say about resurrection in the sense that Christians normally think of it. There is no directly parallel example of an individual being raised by God from the dead with the significance that the resurrection of Jesus was later to have in the New Testament. Concepts of life and death, life after death, immortality, judgment, punishment, and vindication were, of course, rife in both the Jewish and the pagan worlds and certainly fed into the claim by Christians that Jesus had been raised from the dead. But there was no systematic doctrine or philosophy of resurrection which Christians took over from Judaism.

Even so, it is worth noting briefly some of the relatively few Jewish texts that refer to survival of death in one way or another. First, there are texts in which death is avoided by an important figure who is simply "taken up" into heaven, e.g., Enoch (cf. Gen.

5:24) and Elijah (2 Kings 2:1–15); second, occasions when an individual figure is raised from the dead, e.g., the widow of Zarephath's son (1 Kings 17:17–24); the Shunammite woman's son (2 Kings 4:31–37); and the man at Elisha's grave (2 Kings 13:20–21); and third, and more important in many ways, resurrection imagery used to refer to the restoration of Judah or Israel as a nation, e.g., the Valley of Dry Bones (Ezek. 37), and Israel's restoration after involvement in the Syro-Ephraimite war (Hos. 6:1–3). This notion of national resurrection is an important part of the apocalyptic Judaism of the centuries before Jesus. Indeed, it is largely in apocalyptic literature that resurrection imagery first appears (cf. Dan. 12:1–3; Is. 26:19; and also in 2 Maccabees 7).

All of these latter texts are concerned in some way with the survival of death, but they are not specifically concerned with the survival of human beings as such, and in any case they tell us nothing about the nature of the bodies raised.

Although such texts influenced the Christian notion of the resurrection of Jesus, the Christian experience of resurrection was radically new. What did Christians claim had happened in Jesus' resurrection, and what sort of a body did he have? In order to answer these questions we must turn first to the earliest New Testament account of the resurrection of Jesus.

1 Corinthians 15

First Corinthians 15 contains the earliest New Testament material on the resurrection of Jesus. The letter was probably written by Paul from Ephesus in the early to mid-50s of the first century CE. According to Acts 18, Paul had been in Corinth for about eighteen months and then left. Subsequently his authority had deteriorated, and division and disunity had arisen in the community. In particular, a gnostic element had crept into the life and theology of the Corinthian Christians; they had come to value the spirit more than the body; and they had come to emphasize the abstract spiritual realities of the resurrection at the expense of the physical.

Paul's first letter to them deals with a whole range of theological, moral, and practical problems which they were facing and which they had apparently themselves raised with him. He now responds to them in a number of different ways, focusing his strategy on the message of the crucified Christ. Chapter 15 of the letter forms the climax and provides a substantial chapter on Paul's theology of the resurrection. Our main concern here is with 1 Corinthians 15:3–11, which includes the list of people to whom Christ appeared. Paul tells us first how he has received from the tradition what he now relates (cf. 11:23); then we read of Christ's death for sins committed and his resurrection in accordance with scripture; and of the appearances (different from those in the Gospels) to Cephas, the twelve, to more than five hundred at one time, to James, and finally to Paul (cf. Acts 9; 22; 26). It is interesting to note that there is no story of the empty tomb in 1 Corinthians 15. The rest of the chapter then comprises Paul's response to the appearances he has related and to the Corinthians' wider problems over the nature of the resurrection.

The logic of Paul's approach here arises out of a basic misunderstanding on the part of the Corinthians. Apparently they were denying the general resurrection of Christians from the dead, not the resurrection of Christ himself as is often supposed. They affirmed the reality of Christ's resurrection but in a spiritualized, gnostic sense that devalued its physical dimension and disconnected it from their own physical resurrection at the end of time. The famous verse 13 tells of the central connection: "if there is no resurrection of the dead, then Christ has not been raised . . . and your faith is in vain." The issue at stake was really that of the physical nature of the resurrection and its full scope and effect on general Christian resurrection. The remainder of chapter 15 is an argument rooting resurrection in creation and history, linking it up with Adam and humanity generally, and drawing out its full eschatological implications.

What, then, does Paul actually say in 1 Corinthians 15 about the resurrection body of Jesus? In order to answer this question, we must focus on two key Greek words that he uses. Basically, Paul says that Christ "was raised" (v. 4) and "appeared" (v. 5) to the people. These two expressions are crucial in trying to understand what Paul says and turn out to be almost technical terms in his theology of the resurrection. Let us take them in turn.

First, the Greek word *egegertai* which Paul uses in verse 4 is usually translated "he was raised." It probably comes from the tradition that Paul has received and is probably, therefore, one of the earliest words ever used of the resurrection of Jesus. The verb basically has to do with "waking up" and "rousing from sleep." Particularly important in relation to the use here is the word's passive form. The translation is thus "he was raised," that is, "by God." C. F. Evans has commented that "resurrection" is, therefore, a "God word" rather than a "Jesus word." Paul also uses the word *anistemi*, which means "being put back on one's feet" or "being made to stand up." Both words are used metaphorically of the waking of the dead. In 1 Corinthians 15:6 Paul refers to the dead as those who "have fallen asleep." Here the word is *ekoimethesan*, which signifies falling asleep. Thus, at the heart of Paul's claims about the resurrection of Jesus we have several words that have to do with sleeping, waking, and standing up. They are metaphors used by Paul in order to speak of the resurrection of Jesus.

The second key Greek word used by Paul is *ophthe*, which is usually translated "he appeared." Its passive form has the sense of "he was seen" or "he let himself be seen." This could obviously also mean "he showed himself." The Septuagint uses this word to refer to things that were hidden but are now seen and also to people who allow themselves to be seen. It also uses the word of divine appearances. In the New Testament *ophthe* is used, e.g., in Mark 9:4 at the appearance of Elijah and Moses at the transfiguration; in Acts 2:3 at the appearance of tongues of fire at Pentecost; and in John 20:18, 25, 29. It certainly has the sense of revelation, but the appearances also include the participation of those who see. The word thus implies action on the part of the one who is seen but also on the part of those who see. The issue here, then, is also one of perception; it is to do with what appears and what is perceived. But what is it that is seen by those who perceive in the case of the resurrection? What sort of a body is it?

Later in 1 Corinthians 15, Paul explains that there are many different types of body in creation. There are the bodies of men, animals, birds, and fish; and there are celestial and terrestrial bodies (v. 39f.), all of which have a different sort of "glory." There is also the resurrection body with its own glory (v. 42f.). The resurrection body, Paul says, is fundamentally a *soma pneumatikos* or "spiritual body" (v. 44), although it is difficult to establish exactly what he means by this. Paul's words have provoked many different responses from readers, some emphasizing the word "spiritual" more than the word "body." But the latter is precisely the opposite of Paul's intention in 1 Corinthians, where he is reacting to a popular spiritualizing of all things including the resurrection. But the "spiritual body" is not just a physical body either. Paul's emphasis here is on the spiritual and the physical together: the resurrection body is a "spiritual body," a coming together of the physical and the spiritual in God's purposes in Jesus.

Paul's teaching on the resurrection in 1 Corinthians, then, is that Jesus "was raised" from the dead by God. In trying to articulate the experience, Paul speaks of Jesus using metaphors of waking from sleep and standing up. Even though there have been many conflicting interpretations of Paul's words here, part of his claim seems to be that the resurrection body of Jesus was neither merely spiritual nor merely physical: it involved the coming together of the two elements in an ambiguous relation that also involved the perception of those to whom he "appeared." The spiritual and the physical had come together in Jesus' resurrection, and this was related to the general resurrection of the Corinthians from the dead and to the ultimate purposes of God for them at the end of time. With all this in mind, let us turn to the accounts of the resurrection of Jesus in the four canonical Gospels.

The Four Gospels

When we turn to the four canonical Gospels, we find a resurrection tradition rather different from that of 1 Corinthians 15. For a start, the Gospels are narrative rather than discourse, although there are overlapping themes and emphases in the content. It is also noticeable from a single reading that the four Gospels themselves contain very different resurrection stories, although again we shall find significant overlapping emphases. The main texts here are Mark 16:1–8; Matthew 28; Luke 24; and John 20–21. Let us look closely at the main subsections and emphases of these in turn. What do they tell us about Jesus' resurrection body? And what relation do they have theologically to Paul's views in 1 Corinthians?

(a) Mark 16:1–8

In Mark's resurrection narrative, there is only an empty tomb story. It carries many of the characteristic theological features of Mark's Gospel as a whole, especially fear, amazement, and silence. Mark's narrative includes three women at the tomb bringing spices for anointing; the three-day tradition; the youth in white; the message to the disciples and Peter; and the orientation to Galilee. There are no resurrection appearances in Mark, although the so-called longer ending (vv. 9–19), written later, has some. The sense in Mark is one of the stark, frightening activity of God in silence and emptiness. We learn nothing here about the nature of Jesus' resurrection body.

(b) Matthew 28

Matthew's resurrection narrative provides a significant development of Mark, and his own additions and emphases are clear. The subsections of Matthew 28 are: verses 1–10 (the empty tomb); verses 11–15 (the bribing of the guard); and verses 16–20 (an appearance on a mountain in Galilee). Matthew takes over

Mark's basic empty tomb story and embellishes it with dramatic detail so that the effect in the end is really rather different. He also adds a resurrection appearance text in which Jesus appears on a mountain in Galilee. This latter forms the climax to the whole Gospel. In his empty tomb story Matthew omits the plan of the women to anoint the body of Jesus. He adds an earthquake and the appearance of an angel who rolls back the stone. An apocalyptic drama is underway here, and the angel's "appearance was like lightning, and his raiment white as snow" (v. 3). The angel speaks to the women in words similar to those in Mark, and there is the orientation to Galilee. In considerable contrast to the silence of the women in Mark, the women in Matthew leave with fear and joy and go and tell the disciples what has happened. The tale of the bribing of the guard is significant because it shows Matthew defending the physical resurrection of Jesus and refuting the story of the stealing of his body. The major climactic ending of Matthew contains all the strands of theological concern that have grown throughout this Gospel. It also looks out beyond the confines of Judaism to "all the nations" and into the future. The setting on a mountain in Galilee brings to a climax a series of mountains in Matthew that draw distinctly on the Sinai and Zion traditions of Israel's history and literature, and symbolize Torah, covenant, revelation, and eschatology (cf. 4:8; 5:1; 8:1; 15:29; 17:1, 9; 24:3). There is also a strong ecclesial content here when the disciples are commissioned to make more disciples and baptize. The risen Jesus is now a figure of worship, though some doubt. His permanent presence with them is secured into the future until the end of time. Matthew's emphasis in his resurrection narratives is on the risen Jesus' continuing presence with his disciples until the close of the age. The resurrection of Jesus is an earth-shattering physical event grounded in the present, but with a permanent impact ahead into the future. To a significant degree, then, there is an emphasis on the physicality of the resurrection body.

(c) Luke 24

What does Luke add to the picture? The subsections of Luke 24 are: verses 1–12 (empty tomb); verses 13–35 (the Road to Emmaus); verses 36–43 (eating broiled fish); verses 44–49 (interpreting the scriptures); and verses 50–53 (the ascension). As is frequently pointed out, Luke's resurrection events are all based in the Jerusalem area. This gives a particular theological thrust to his resurrection narrative as a whole. The resurrection events occur in the city in which God has already revealed himself to his people over the centuries. Then, the Gospel is to go forward from Jerusalem, ultimately to Rome (in Acts). Galilee is a thing of the past (v. 6). It is here in Luke, however, that we also begin to learn more about the nature of the resurrection body itself. Like Mark and Matthew, Luke has an empty tomb story in which he basically follows Mark, although he emphasizes the empty tomb more: "they did not find the body" (v. 3). In Luke, the women enter the tomb before encountering two men who ask them about seeking the living among the dead. There is the orientation to Galilee, with detail about Jesus' crucifixion. As in Matthew, the women tell the disciples about the resurrection.

The major addition in Luke is the Emmaus story, a tightly compact narrative that pretty well says everything Luke has to say about the resurrection of Jesus. It is, therefore, worth some attention. Based in the vicinity of Jerusalem, the story has Jesus "draw near" alongside two travelers. He comes to them in their conversation but they do not recognize him. From this it is instantly clear that the risen body of Jesus is not identical with his body before the resurrection. Major themes of Lukan christology appear in this passage, including Jesus' status as a prophet and the importance of his saving death. Once again, Luke emphasizes the emptiness of the tomb: they "did not find his body" (v. 23). The significance of Jesus' death is then seen in relation to the fulfillment of scripture (vv. 27, 44–49). In a dramatic meal scene evoking the eucharist,

Jesus is finally recognized but immediately disappears. When the disciples return again to Jerusalem the proclamation is that "the Lord has risen indeed, and has appeared to Simon!" (v. 34), a detail found only in Luke. The final sections of Luke 24 further emphasize the physical reality of the resurrection: "See my hands and my feet . . . handle me" (v. 39), and Jesus eats a piece of fish (v. 43). The significant contribution of Luke here is twofold: he insists upon the physical reality of the resurrection on the one hand, but also emphasizes a clear difference or ambiguity with regard to Jesus' physical appearance, on the other. Jesus is not straightforwardly recognizable but is certainly physically risen.

(d) John 20–21

When we turn to the Fourth Gospel, the texts are completely different. The subsections of John 20–21 are: 20:1–10 (empty tomb); verses 11–18 (appearance to Mary Magdalene); verses 19–25 (breathing the Holy Spirit); verses 26–29 (appearance to Thomas); verses 30–31 (a statement of purpose from the author); and 21:1–14 (appearance in Galilee); verses 15–23 (commissioning Peter); and verses 24–25 (redactional closure). These narratives incorporate the following main features: the third day tradition; one woman instead of three; the stone rolled away (and not mentioned previously in the story); two angels in the tomb; Peter and the beloved disciple together, but Peter is the first to believe (20:1f.; cf. 13:23; 18:15); seeing and believing (20:8, 25; cf. 4:48; 6:30); calling Mary by name (cf. 10:3, 14f.); Jesus' ascent to the Father, exaltation and lifting up (20:17; cf. 3:13–15; 6:62; 8:28; 12:32; 14:12, 28); fear of the Jews (20:19; cf. 7:13; 19:38); peace (20:19, 21, 26; cf. 14:27; 16:33); Jesus' hands and side (20:20, 25, 27; cf. 19:34; Luke 24:39); and mission based on sending of the son by the father (20:21; cf. 17:18).

More significantly for our purposes, there are parallels and significant theological overlap between John 20 and 21 and Luke 24. Some commentators have thought that Luke and John may have worked with common sources in their passion narratives, and there is certainly a similarity of theological outlook here in their resurrection narratives. One important feature occurs immediately in the christophany to Mary Magdalene, who is now the central character in an empty tomb story quite different from Mark, Matthew, and Luke. When the risen Jesus appears, Mary does not recognize him until he speaks her name (cf. 10:3, 14f.). His physical body is apparently different from what it had been before. This turns out to be a key element in the Johannine perspective, and we find the same element of ambiguity in Jesus' identity that we found in Luke. It is also interesting to note that the Fourth Gospel uses the word *heoraka* here (20:18, 25, 29), which is related to the word *ophthe* used by Paul in 1 Corinthians 15. For John and for Luke, then, the overall message is twofold: on the one hand, the risen Jesus is not immediately recognizable at the physical level and can appear through closed doors (20:26). He has not simply come back from the dead, and the moments of recognition are dependent upon other factors like hearing one's name or believing. But on the other hand, there is stress on the physical nature of the resurrection: the grave cloths are lying empty (20:5–7), and Thomas is in principle able to put his finger into Jesus' side, although we are not actually told that he does so (20:27). In Luke and John, an anti-docetic emphasis on the physical nature of the resurrection is combined with the theme of difficulty of recognizing that body. The similarity here with Paul's "spiritual body" is striking: the resurrection body is at once spiritual and physical.

So what does the New Testament contribute to the ongoing debates about the resurrection of Jesus? What exactly does it claim about Jesus' resurrection body? The background to the resurrection in ancient Judaism is thin, although it is clear that resurrection imagery emerged from the apocalyptic Judaism of the centuries immediately preceding Jesus. The Christian experience of Jesus' resurrection, however, was something radically new. In the earliest text on the resurrection, 1 Corinthians 15, Paul writes of Jesus being raised by God (*egegertai*) and of his appearing or being seen (*ophthe*) by particular people. He uses a sleep metaphor indicating that resurrection is a "waking up" from the dead. For Paul, Jesus' resurrection body is a "spiritual body" (*soma pneumatikos*), an expression that indicates a combination of the spiritual and physical in the purposes of God in raising Jesus. In Mark's Gospel there is an empty tomb story, although we learn nothing there of the nature of Jesus' resurrection body, while Matthew has an emphasis on the physical resurrection.

It is in the Gospels of Luke and John, however, that we find themes closely relating to Paul. In the Road to Emmaus story in Luke and in the appearance of Jesus to Mary Magdalene and to Thomas in John, Jesus' resurrection body is unrecognizable by the disciples until they come to "see" him in particular situations. It is, however, also emphasized that Jesus' risen body is a physical body.

In all, the central message of the New Testament writers concerning the resurrection of Jesus, especially as found in Paul, Luke, and John, is that the "spiritual body" of Jesus was neither merely physical nor merely spiritual, neither a corpse nor a ghost, but spirit and matter working together in the purposes of God.

EPILOGUE

I hope that in reading *The Gospels Today: Challenging Readings of John, Mark, Luke & Matthew*, you have gained a good sense of some of the things that are going on in the world of Gospel studies today, and that you have come to see the New Testament Gospels and especially the texts discussed in these chapters in a new light. In the last century and a half of critical study of the Gospels there has been a great deal of development in understanding the world in which the Gospels were written, how they came to be written, and of how particular Gospel texts might be understood and interpreted. The revolution caused by the various quests for the historical Jesus along with archaeological discoveries and the appearance of many different methods of studying the Gospel texts have all changed scholars' perceptions of what the Gospels are.

I am convinced that the scholarly work that has been done should now find its way beyond universities and colleges into more general use in church study groups, bible classes, and sermons. So, I hope that the chapters in this volume have enabled you to appreciate something of the constructive difference critical study of the Gospels can make.

The chapters in this volume should have set you off on a journey of rereading the Gospels. Critical analysis of biblical texts can so often illuminate the meaning of the text concerned and at the same time yield positive theological results. I think this can be seen to be the case in these essays. I hope that they have opened new doors for you in appreciating the depth and complexity of the selected texts. Thus, the long hard look at the Prologue to John's Gospel revealed just how rich a theology lies in its verses and how important a theology of creation is to its writer. To see just how the mind of the writer of an ancient text works and how this process might nurture contemporary theology is informative and exciting in so many different ways. The debate about where Jesus was born may not have produced any final answers, but I hope it took you into the historical context of his birth and into the nativity narratives of Matthew and Luke in ways that you may not have encountered before. Whatever else, it pointed up the various sides in the debate and what the different options amount to. As you have seen, I personally think that it is quite possible that Jesus was born in Bethlehem of Judea.

The discussion of Jesus the prophet was enlightening in a different way. Few Christians these days think of Jesus primarily as a prophet, but I have shown how important it is to see him as standing in line with the great prophets of ancient Israel and as a spokesman for social justice in his own world. This helps to recover something of a sense of who he really was and what he stood for in his own day. The debate over the titles "son of god" and "son of man" will undoubtedly continue, but I hope I've shown at least some of the complexity of the background of these titles and that they didn't originally mean what they so often mean on the lips of modern Christians. The chapter on the so-called Messianic Secret in Mark's Gospel should have enabled you to engage with a great deal of the narrative of that Gospel. I hope that the discussion helped you to appreciate not only something about a single theme in Mark but also to see the whole Gospel as rooted in apophatic or negative theology.

Probably one of the most challenging chapters in this volume was "Jesus the Bread of God." For many Christians, the words in John's Gospel about eating Christ's flesh and drinking his blood are fundamentally bound up with the eucharist. As I have shown, however, when you look at that passage closely it is easy to see that the emphasis is on Jesus himself rather than on the eucharist. Furthermore, I hope that the material on metaphor in that chapter helped readers to see how metaphors work and how they achieve their meaning, especially in John 6. The importance of metaphor has been emphasized in almost every academic discipline in recent years, and it would be irresponsible to leave metaphor out of a discussion of Jesus the Bread of Life.

On another note, the parables of Jesus have been read and interpreted in many different ways over the centuries. Every teacher and preacher is faced sooner or later with the need to interpret a parable of Jesus. I hope you have seen that the Parable of the Prudent Steward, as I prefer to call it, is a classic test case for the would-be parable interpreter. Almost every word and phrase in the parable is open to different interpretations, and the notion that a parable has only one meaning waiting to be found in the text is unrealistic and unhelpful. I hope that this chapter provided you with something of a methodological test case for parable interpretation. The Stilling of the Storm story from the synoptic Gospels is one of the most beautiful in the Gospel tradition, but it is so often read simply as a "miracle story" with no further investigation into its meaning. I have tried to bring out just how much the background of this text needs to be considered if its full theological meaning is to be appreciated. The significance of the story for modern "creation theologies," rooted as it is in ancient Near-Eastern creation stories, is considerable.

Finally, I hope you have gained new insights into the Transfiguration and Resurrection of Jesus through the last two chapters of this book. The Transfiguration has so often been seen as just another Resurrection appearance story, but I have shown how important it is to see it, like so many other texts, in its full context in the Gospel narrative. The surrounding texts concerning the suffering of the Son of Man provide an important part of the backdrop to the Transfiguration itself and show that the theology of Transfiguration focuses on the transfiguration of suffering rather than just pointing forward to the Resurrection. In this sense the Transfiguration story has a theological significance way beyond the narratives in which it is found.

I hope that the final chapter, on the Resurrection itself, helped you to look again at the four resurrection narratives in the Gospels. So often these texts are taken for granted, and even scholars and preachers can become overfamiliar with them. I hope that the discussion of the differences between the four accounts alerted you to the key theological emphases in each Gospel. Hopefully also the discussion of the "spiritual body" in that chapter drew your attention to an important and neglected feature of Resurrection theology.

Overall, I hope that this second volume of *The Gospels Today* has opened some important doors for you in reading the Gospels. I hope it has encouraged you to look again at some key Gospel passages and enabled you to appreciate some of the important issues that arise in studying Gospel texts in detail. Many different books have been written on how to read the Gospels, and there is a wide variety of approaches to texts, but I hope that these essays have provided you with some new insights and provoked some new thoughts. I also hope they have demonstrated the fact that serious critical investigation into Gospel texts can produce important historical and theological results that are of lasting value. Whether you use these essays in preparation for assignments, examinations, discussions, sermons, or privately for your own purposes, I hope you will continue to find them interesting and helpful. Finally, I hope this volume has inspired you to make further inquiries into the Gospels in the future.

BIBLIOGRAPHY

GENERAL SOURCES

Introductions

Brown, Raymond E. *Introduction to the New Testament*. New York: Doubleday, 1997.

Johnson, Luke Timothy. *The Writings of the New Testament: An Interpretation*. Revised Edition Plus CD-ROM of Full Text and Study Tools. Minneapolis: Augsburg Fortress, 2002.

Ehrman, Bart D. *The New Testament: An Historical Introduction to the Early Christian Writings.* Oxford: Oxford University Press, 2003.

Dictionaries

Coggins, R. J. and J. L. Houlden (eds.). *A Dictionary of Biblical Interpretation*. London: SCM, 1990.

Freedman, David Noel (ed.). *The Anchor Bible Dictionary*. New York: Doubleday, 1992, six volumes.

Metzger, Bruce M. and Michael D. Coogan. *The Oxford Companion of the Bible*. Oxford: Oxford University Press, 1993.

Commentaries on the Gospels

Barton, John and John Muddiman (eds.). *The Oxford Bible Commentary*. Oxford: Oxford University Press, 2001. Also available on CD-ROM.

Beare, Francis Wright. *The Gospel According to Matthew*. Oxford: Blackwell, 1981.

Brown, R. E. *The Gospel According to John 1–X11*. New York: Doubleday, 1966.

Davies, W. D. and D. C. Allison. *A Critical and Exegetical Commentary on the Gospel According to Saint Matthew*. 3 vols. Edinburgh: T&T Clark, 1991.

Evans, C. F. *Saint Luke*. London: SCM, 1990.

Green, Joel B. *The Gospel of Luke*. Grand Rapids: Eerdmans, 1997.

Hooker, Morna D. *The Gospel According to St. Mark*. London: A&C Black, 1991.

Keener, Craig S. *A Commentary on the Gospel of Matthew*. Grand Rapids: Eerdmans, 1999.

Maloney, Francis J. *The Gospel of Mark: A Commentary*. Peabody, MA: Hendrickson, 2002.

Marshall, I. Howard. *The Gospel of Luke: A Commentary on the Greek Text*. London: Paternoster, 1978.

Ridderbos, Herman. *The Gospel of John: A Theological Commentary*. Grand Rapids: Erdmans, 1997.

Witherington III, Ben. *The Gospel of Mark: A Socio-Rhetorical Commentary*. Grand Rapids: Eerdmans, 2001.

Witherington III, Ben. *John's Wisdom: A Commentary on the Fourth Gospel*. Louisville: Westminster John Knox, 1995.

Web Page

See www.ntgateway.com for a lively and comprehensive array of New Testament resources.

CHAPTER BY CHAPTER

1. Rereading the Prologue

Dunn, James D. G. *Christology in the Making: An Inquiry into the Origins of the Doctrine of the Incarnation*. London: SCM, 1980.

Edwards, Ruth. *Discovering John*. London: SPCK, 2003.

Käsemann, Ernst. "The Structure and Purpose of the Prologue to John's Gospel," in *New Testament Questions of Today*. London: SCM, 1969.
Robinson, John A. T. "The Relation of the Prologue to the Gospel of St. John," in *Twelve More New Testament Studies*. London: SCM, 1984.
Sanders, Jack T. *The New Testament Christological Hymns: Their Historical Religious Background*. Cambridge: Cambridge University Press, 1971.
Scott, Martin. *Sophia and the Johannine Jesus*. JSNTSS, 71, Sheffield: Sheffield Academic Press, 1992.

2. Bethlehem

Brown, Raymond E. *The Birth of the Messiah: A Commentary on the Infancy Narratives in Matthew and Luke*. London: Geoffrey Chapman, 1977.
Farris, Stephen. *The Hymns of Luke's Infancy Narratives: Their Origin, Meaning and Significance*. Sheffield: Sheffield Academic Press, 1985.
Freed, Edwin D. *The Stories of Jesus' Birth: A Critical Introduction*. Sheffield: Sheffield Academic Press, 2001.
Sherwin-White, A. N. *Roman Society and Roman Law in the New Testament*. Oxford: Clarendon, 1963.
Taylor, Joan. *Christians and the Holy Places*. Oxford: Clarendon, 1993.
Ramsay, W. M. *Was Christ Born at Bethlehem?* London: Hodder & Stoughton, 1898.

3. More Than a Prophet?

Aune, David. *Prophecy in Early Christianity and the Ancient Mediterranean World*. Grand Rapids: Eerdmans, 1983.
Barton, John. *Oracles of God*. London: Darton, Longman & Todd, 1986.
Dodd, C. H. "Jesus as Teacher and Prophet," in *Mysterium Christi*, ed. G. K. A. Bell and Adolf Deissmann. London, New York, Toronto: Longmans, Green & Co., 1930, pp. 53–66.
Hooker, Morna. *The Signs of a Prophet: The Prophetic Actions of Jesus*. London: SCM, 1997.
Lindblom, J. *Prophecy in Ancient Israel*. Philadelphia: Fortress, 1962.
Witherington III, Ben. *Jesus the Seer: The Progress of Prophecy*. Peabody, MA: Hendrickson, 1999.

4. Son of God and Son of Man

Brown, Raymond E. *An Introduction to New Testament Christology.* Mahwah, NJ: Paulist Press, 1994.

Casey, Maurice. *The Son of Man: The Interpretation and Influence of Daniel* 7. London: SPCK, 1980.

Dunn, J. D. G. *Christology in the Making: An Inquiry into the Origins of the Doctrine of the Incarnation*. London: SCM, 1980.

Dunn, J. D. G. *Jesus Remembered* (*Christianity in the Making*, vol. 1). Grand Rapids: Eerdmans, 2003.

Hurtado, Larry. *Lord Jesus Christ: Devotion to Jesus in Earliest Christianity.* Grand Rapids: Eerdmans, 2003.

Lindars, Barnabas. *Jesus: Son of Man*. London: SPCK, 1983.

5. Messianic Mystery

Magness, J. Lee. *Sense and Absence: Structure and Suspension in the Ending of Mark's Gospel*. Atlanta: Scholars Press, 1986.

Matera, Frank J. *What Are They Saying about Mark?* New York: Paulist, 1987.

Telford, W. R. *The Theology of the Gospel of Mark*. Cambridge: Cambridge University Press, 1999.

Thompson, Mary R. *The Role of Disbelief in Mark: A New Approach to the Second Gospel*. New York: Paulist, 1989.

Weeden, Theodore J. *Mark: Traditions in Conflict*. Philadelphia: Fortress, 1971.

Wrede, Wilhelm. *The Messianic Secret*. London and Cambridge: James Clarke, 1971.

6. Jesus the Bread of God

Borgen, Peder. *Bread from Heaven: An Exegetical Study of the Concept of Manna in the Gospel of John and the Writings of Philo*. Leiden: Brill, 1965.

Hawkes, Terence. *Metaphor*. London: Methuen, 1972.

McFague, Sallie. *Metaphorical Theology: Models of God in Religious Language*. Philadelphia: Fortress, 1982.

Soskice, Janet Martin. *Metaphor and Religious Language*. Oxford: Clarendon, 1985.

Stiver, Dan. *The Philosophy of Religious Language: Sign, Symbol and Story.* Oxford: Blackwell, 1995.

Webster, Jane S. *Ingesting Jesus: Eating and Drinking in the Gospel of John.* Atlanta: Society of Biblical Literature, 2003.

7. The Parable of the Prudent Steward

Bailey, K. E. *Poet and Peasant: A Literary Cultural Approach to the Parables in Luke.* Grand Rapids: Eerdmans, 1976.

Derrett, J. D. M. "The Parable of the Unjust Steward," in *Law in the New Testament.* London: Darton, Longman & Todd, 1970.

Flusser, David. "The Parable of the Unjust Steward: Jesus' Criticism of the Essenes," in James Charlesworth (ed.), *Jesus and the Dead Sea Scrolls.* New York: Doubleday, 1992.

Nickle, Keith F. *Preaching the Gospel of Luke: Proclaiming God's Royal Rule.* Louisville: Westminster John Knox, 2000.

Reid, Barbara E. *Parables for Preachers.* Collegeville, MN: Liturgical Press, 2000.

Robinson, John. *The Roots of a Radical.* London: SCM, 1980, pp. 135–39.

8. Stilling the Storm

Bornkamm, Günther. "The Stilling of the Storm in Matthew," in Bornkamm, Günther, Gerhard Barth, and Heinz Joachim Held (eds.), *Tradition and Interpretation in Matthew.* London: SCM, 1963.

Collins, A. Y. *The Combat Myth in the Book of Revelation.* Missoula, MT: Scholars Press, 1976.

Day, John. *God's Conflict with the Dragon and the Sea: Echoes of a Canaanite Myth in the Old Testament.* Cambridge: Cambridge University Press, 1985.

Keller, Ernst and Marie-Louise Keller. *Miracles in Dispute: A Continuing Debate.* London: SCM, 1969.

Simkins, Ronald A. *Creator and Creation: Nature in the Worldview of Ancient Israel.* Peabody, MA: Hendrickson, 1994.

Winton, Thomas, D. (ed.). *Documents from Old Testament Times.* New York: Harper & Row, 1958.

9. Metamorphosis

Donaldson, Terence. *Jesus on the Mountain: A Study in Matthean Theology.* JSNTSS, 8, Sheffield: JSOT Press, 1985.

Lee, Dorothy. *Transfiguration.* London: Continuum, 2005.

Marshall, Bob. *The Transfiguration of Jesus.* London: Darton, Longman & Todd, 1994.

McGuckin, John Anthony. *The Transfiguration of Christ in Scripture and Tradition.* New York: Edwin Mellen, 1986.

Pilch, John J. "The Transfiguration of Jesus: An Experience of Alternate Reality," in Philip Esler (ed.), *Modelling Early Christianity: Social-Scientific Studies of the New Testament in Its Context.* London and New York: Routledge, 1995.

Wilson, Andrew. *Transfigured: A Derridean Re-Reading of the Markan Transfiguration.* Edinburgh: T&T Clark, 2006.

10. Resurrection

Barton, S. and Stanton, G. *Resurrection: Essays in Honour of Leslie Houlden.* London: SPCK, 1994.

Catchpole, David. *Resurrection People: Studies in the Resurrection Narratives of the Gospels.* London: Darton, Longman & Todd, 2000.

Perkins, Pheme. *Resurrection: New Testament Witness and Contemporary Reflection.* London: Geoffrey Chapman, 1984.

Stewart, Robert B. *The Resurrection of Jesus: John Dominic Crossan and N. T. Wright in Dialogue.* Philadelphia: Fortress, 2006.

Wedderburn, A. J. M. *Beyond Resurrection.* London: SCM, 1999.

Wright, N. T. *The Resurrection of the Son of God.* London: SPCK, 2003.

INDEX

ABOUT THE AUTHOR

Stephen W. Need was born in Nottingham, UK. He received his Ph.D. in Systematic Theology from King's College London and has taught New Testament Studies in Chichester, Southampton, and Jerusalem. He has traveled widely in the Middle East and is currently dean of St. George's College Jerusalem.